Effective Evangelism
A Theological Mandate

"No one in the world of missions today is so profound a thinker, so traveled an investigator, so fearless a critic, or so constructive a force as Donald McGavran. These lectures throw down the gauntlet to today's Christian leaders, theologians, and executives like no other book. What a bold challenge, what a fascinating biographical approach, based on ninety years of perceptive existence!"

—Ralph D. Winter

"In a day of great opportunity for world evangelization—and no little confusion as to the nature of our mission—I [would] urge evangelical divinity schools and theological seminaries to read what Dr. McGavran has to say and to give serious consideration to following his primary suggestions."

—David J. Hesselgrave

"No church will enjoy the blessing of God when it forgets its evangelistic imperative. Tragically, however, many pastors have had little training to equip them effectively for this vital task. Ironically, the majority of theological seminaries and Bible colleges in America have relegated courses in evangelism to a secondary status in the curriculum—or even oblivion. Now Donald McGavran has set forth a bold and yet simple proposal to make required courses in evangelism a central part of every minister's education. His proposal would not only revolutionize theological education, but could bring new vision and vitality to the churches of America. I heartily endorse his proposal."

—Billy Graham

". . . an outstanding contribution to the evangelical divinity schools and theological seminaries of America."

—Elmer L. Towns

"As the founder of the School of World Mission and 'Father of Church Planting,' Dr. McGavran has served on the faculty of nine theological seminaries and lectured in many more. . . . He has interacted with and shared ideas and theological truths with thousands of Christian leaders during a long and rich ministry for our Lord. He is quite likely the most qualified man in the entire world to write on this extremely important subject."

—William R. Bright

Effective Evangelism
A Theological Mandate

Donald A. McGavran

Presbyterian and Reformed Publishing Company
Phillipsburg, New Jersey

Unless otherwise indicated, Scripture quotations are from the New International Version.

Manufactured in the United States of America

Library of Congress Cataloging-in-Publication Data

McGavran, Donald Anderson, 1897–
  Effective evangelism.

  Includes bibliographical references and index.
  1. Church growth. 2. Church growth—Study and
teaching. 3. Evangelistic work. 4. Evangelistic
work—Study and teaching. I. Title.
BV652.25.M257 1988   266   87–13087
ISBN 0–87552–289–0

This book is dedicated to
Betty Ann Klebe
to whom I am deeply indebted
for her invaluable assistance
in the preparation of the manuscript.

Contents

Foreword

This book may send shock waves through the halls of Christian colleges and seminaries. Liberal and conservative schools alike come under indictment, as Donald McGavran, the dean of modern evangelical missiologists, examines the strengths and weaknesses of theological institutions in the area of evangelism and calls for a serious reprioritizing of theological curricula. If the author's arguments are accepted and his proposals applied, the growth patterns of Christ's church throughout the world are likely to be dramatically improved.

McGavran argues that theological institutions should accept responsibility for training tomorrow's leaders for ministry in the real world, the world in which over two billion people still need to be reached with the gospel and millions are adrift in a sea of secularism and religious confusion. He pleads for curricular revisions of a kind that will make the effective communication of God's Word and the multiplication of viable churches a substantial and required part of every school's program.

This is a theological issue, McGavran maintains, because the God of the Bible who is the object of true theological study is the God who has revealed His missionary intention for all races and peoples of the earth. God wants the world evangelized and discipled, and to study theology in a way that misses or minimizes this point is to adopt and perpetuate a distorted view of God and is, in effect, a heresy.

The chapters of this book were first presented as lectures at Westminster Theological Seminary in Philadelphia. This seminary, like many others, is increasingly aware of the need for greater integration between evangelism and the other departments of theological education. Awed by the rapid growth of non-Christian populations and the burgeoning cities, and sensitive to the fact that theological education must be geared to the needs of churches-in-mission, Westminster invited Dr. McGavran to spell out for faculty and students the implications of a mission-oriented curriculum that would produce effective communicators of the gospel in this country and abroad. His analysis and challenge to the seminary, presented now in this volume, should be taken seriously by every institution that trains workers for Christ's kingdom.

Woven throughout the book is the story of McGavran's own pilgrimage as the founder of the church growth school of missiology and the struggles through which he and his coworkers passed as they defined effective evangelism in terms of the multiplication of living, growing churches. They confronted opposition from the theological left, which did not share their commitment to the authority of the biblical mandate, and from the conservative right, which felt threatened by the constant demand for accountability in terms of measurable church multiplication.

Basic to the church growth understanding of the missionary mandate is a firm commitment to the authority of Scripture. A major reason, says McGavran, for today's vast indifference to evangelism and church growth is the prevalent low view of Scripture. Wherever the authority of Scripture has eroded, the church loses its power and the call to biblical mission falls on deaf ears. God's command to proclaim the gospel to *panta ta ethne*, leading them to obedience of faith, is of importance only to those who hold to the inspired and utterly dependable Word of God, the ultimate authority for faith and practice. In schools and churches where the Word is loved and honored, the urgency of winning the lost will be felt by professors, ministers, and lay people alike.

Biblical soundness, however, does not by itself guarantee healthy church growth. There is a kind of biblical soundness that focuses exclusive attention on particular doctrines and interprets them in such a way that they have little bearing on evangelism. Even spiritual renewal, which is the desire and concern of many churches today, will not translate into church growth if the focus of renewal is mainly in terms of the existing congregation and its activities within the church building.

At the same time, biblical soundness of the kind that recognizes the missionary intention of the God who saves sinners through His Son and who sends the church on a redemptive mission to the world certainly will produce healthy growth and robust churches. Likewise, spiritual renewal that sees Christians recommitting themselves to living the life of the Spirit under the direction of the Word will burst through old social and cultural barriers and lead to a greater harvest of souls and discipling of many segments of society, as well as a host of new ministries to the needy and oppressed. In the biblical balance of doctrinal soundness, spiritual renewal, and evangelistic outreach lies the secret of growth and effective ministry.

Theological schools and Bible colleges can play a vital role in the evangelization of North America and all other nations, says McGavran, if they are willing to make necessary changes in the way they train future leaders. They must rethink their curricula and require that all students take basic courses in evangelism, church growth, and Christian perspectives on the gospel and society. Besides this, they must instill in their students an understanding of Christian vocation that breaks with the traditions preoccupied with the maintenance of beautiful buildings, the niceties of denominational life, and the preaching and hearing of sermons that say little to the uncommitted and unconverted.

From the perspective of a seminary teacher and mission executive who listens regularly to the complaints and cries for help of church members in this country and abroad, I can think of nothing more needful, indeed, more revolutionary for the church and its theological schools, than the appeal contained in this volume.

Roger S. Greenway

1

Theological Education and Effective Evangelism

Do theological seminaries have anything to do with effective evangelism? Or are seminaries and Bible colleges concerned only with correct views of the Bible and with inculcating true doctrines? Must not a theological seminary deal exclusively with theological concepts required by the Bible? Is not effective evangelism a part of life *outside* the seminary?

Though we might be tempted to separate theological education from evangelism, we are reminded of our eternal God's command to disciple all the peoples of the earth and His promise that in Abraham all the peoples of the world would be blessed. We therefore affirm that seminaries and Bible colleges should do two things. First, train their students to communicate to members of the church correct views of the Bible and correct doctrines. Second, train future ministers to make every congregation they serve evangelistically effective at home and abroad. Effective evangelization is an essential part of correct doctrine.

Most Theological Seminaries Do Not Teach Church Growth or Effective Evangelism

During my lifetime I have served as a faculty member in nine theological seminaries. I have lectured in many more and met many fellow theological professors in several continents. Though I have never done a careful research on the subject, I believe that I am correct when I state that most theological training schools do not count evangelism or church growth an essential part of their curricula. In a few schools a two- or four-hour course on evangelism is an elective. In many, however, no course on effective evangelism is offered.

1

Under the impact of the worldwide church growth movement this regrettable state of affairs is slowly changing. For example, in March of 1983 at Westminster Theological Seminary in Philadelphia forty-eight leaders of the Reformed tradition gathered to discuss reaching the unreached. Inevitably they discussed the theological seminary's place in world evangelization. Professor Harvie M. Conn rendered a notable service to the world church when he published the contributions of nine of the participants under the title, *Reaching the Unreached*. In his foreword Professor Conn asks, "What must be done . . . to mobilize theological seminaries for the work?" He concurs with Addison Soltau's statement that seminaries tend to be "static and isolationist."[1] Quoting Roger S. Greenway, Conn also asks, "Will 'unreached peoples' become another missiological fad if the church remains preoccupied with its own edification and doctrinal purity?"[2] Again Professor Conn asks, "Is our traditional language of 'home' and 'foreign' missions . . . too geographically oriented to find the unevangelized . . . of our own neighborhoods?"[3]

In the chapter titled "Mobilizing the Seminaries," Addison Soltau says, "Seminaries are looked upon as institutions to prepare for the parish ministry, rarely for . . . evangelism."[4] Soltau also says that missions are perceived as having "no rightful place" in a theological seminary "alongside the established disciplines."[5]

This tragic view is held by leaders in other branches of the universal church. For example, Dr. Paul Benjamin, head of the National Church Growth Research Center in Washington, D.C., has some unshakable convictions on exactly this sorry situation. In his 1986 book, *The Vision Splendid: Believing*, he writes:

> I know many ministers who want to become more involved in outreach. However, neither their academic background nor their experience has equipped them for evangelism.

1. Harvie M. Conn, ed., *Reaching the Unreached, The Old-New Challenge* (Phillipsburg, NJ: Presbyterian and Reformed, 1984), p. viii.
2. Ibid.
3. Ibid.
4. Ibid., p. 152
5. Ibid., p. 153.

Again he says,

> A minister/evangelist must always be conscious of the world
> arena in which the individuals he hopes to win are living. He
> can never bridge the gap between Christians and non-
> Christians by continuing to ignore secular thinkers.[6]

In his entire book Dr. Benjamin insists that every minister shepherd the sheep in his fold *and bring back to the fold multitudes of sheep
who are lost in the wilderness, a prey for wolves and evil men.*

The extraordinary state of affairs discussed in this first chapter is
evidently well known to theological leaders in many branches of the
church. The reason for this regrettable condition is easy to state.
Protestant theological seminaries were born and their curricula fairly
well established in the years 1550–1800. During these years Roman
Catholic mission orders were very active in Latin America, the
Philippine Islands, and a few other sections of the world. But the
Protestants, sealed off by Muslim armies in the south and east and
Spanish and Portuguese navies in the Atlantic to the west, believed
that their main task was Christianization of the masses of nominal
Roman Catholics who had been swept into the Protestant church by
the Reformation.

The concept, therefore, of the theological seminary as an institution that trained ministers to maintain and improve existing churches
became very firmly established. *A maintenance mentality still domi-
nates most seminary faculties.*

Today, however, we look out on a very different world. Christians can reach any part of the world in a matter of a few hours.
Enormous numbers of Americans cross the oceans to visit Europe,
Latin America, Asia, Africa. Citizens of all these different nations
flock to the United States. The concept of one world inhabited by
one great human family is voiced again and again by today's media.
It becomes part of the everyday thinking of most American citizens.

Furthermore, Protestant churches today are led by highly trained
ministers. Most American denominations require that those ordained
be at least college graduates. Many denominations insist that on top

6. Paul Benjamin, *The Vision Splendid: Believing* (Washington, D.C.: American
Press, 1986), preface.

of four years in college there be an additional three or more years in seminary. The Christian minister must be a highly educated man. He must think that way and speak that way. This almost guarantees that he will remain out of touch with blue-collar America and some of white-collar America also.

Today seminary faculties in all six continents look out on a world that is wide open to the gospel. True, some nations are closed to missionaries from any land, but the number of unbelieving, unreached populations open to world evangelization is enormous. The existing evangelistic efforts of most denominations are touching only a fringe of the available populations. Any exact and truthful picture of the spread of the Christian faith indicates that, while in a few places it has spread very greatly, in most places the number of believing, practicing Christians is relatively small. Even in Europe and North America committed Christians are a small proportion of the total population. They will remain a small and sometimes shrinking part unless seminaries begin to train their students in effective evangelism. I repeat—*they will remain a small and sometimes shrinking part unless seminaries begin to train their students in effective evangelism.*

All Seminaries Need to Make Effective Evangelism
A Substantial Part of Their Required Courses

A typical seminary requires thirty-six four-hour courses successfully completed to gain the coveted degree of Bachelor of Divinity or Master of Divinity. Of these thirty-six four-hour courses one may be an elective or very occasionally a required course in evangelism. In most seminaries, however, many complete the Master of Divinity curriculum without learning how to win men and women of their own neighborhoods to Christ. Furthermore, they learn nothing about the world's vast unreached populations of thousands of varieties and multiplying congregations in each.

I am speaking about the seminary world in general. One thirty-sixth of the seminary curriculum (or no evangelism at all) will not satisfy God's will for today. It is not theologically correct. It states a theology that is untrue to eternal God's oft-expressed purpose to seek and save the lost. It is also functionally inadequate. It does not recognize that every American and European minister goes out into a world that is largely secular, humanistic, and often pagan. It does not even see that the European and American world where everyone was once a Christian and had only to be educated no longer exists. Our world population today is only one-quarter even nominally Christian. Tomorrow only one-fifth will call themselves Christian. Practicing Christians are, of course, a much smaller proportion of the total.

As I look at the very complex mosaic of mankind in North America I am sure that one four-hour course could not possibly instruct future ministers in how to reach effectively the multitudinous segments of population they will find in the cities and countrysides where they labor. At one end of the spectrum will be the secularists. Some of these educated men and women follow the religion of scientism. Others are openly agnostic or atheistic. Many believe that God the Father almighty described in the Bible does not exist. At the other end of the spectrum will be the recent immigrants from Asia, Latin America, and Europe.

Add to this picture the fact that ministers in North America face the need for sending missionaries to Asia, Africa, Latin America, and Europe to find the lost there. In France the Roman Catholic Church calls large sections of the nation mission territories, because in them less than 5 percent of the population ever attend mass. Similar statistics could easily be quoted for Roman Catholic and Protestant populations in most other European nations. In Finland less than 5 percent of the population is found in church on Sunday.

This whole unwon population in our own nation and around the world is now immediately accessible. Students in American Bible colleges and seminaries speak English, and English has become during the past fifty years the most widespread language known to man. English is to the latter part of the twentieth century what *koine* Greek was to the apostle Paul. It was in *koine* Greek that he wrote to all the members of ten or more house churches in Corinth, "I am . . . seeking . . . the good of many, so that they may be saved. Follow my example, as I follow the example of Christ" (1 Cor. 10:33–11:1).

Theological seminaries preparing effective ministers of Jesus Christ should pay considerably more attention to how the correct doctrines and the correct Scriptures they must teach can be communicated and believed by multitudes in order to carry out eternal God's command. The minister is a communicator of the gospel. He must know how to evangelize effectively.

Would it not be highly desirable to rule that of the thirty-six four-hour courses required for the Master of Divinity, five be devoted to effective evangelism? The five I suggest are by no means the only possible ones. Each seminary and Bible school would determine five great aspects of effective evangelism that it wanted to teach. Some would emphasize certain aspects of the giant task. Others would emphasize other aspects. However, to make my proposal concrete, let me mention the following five.

The first would teach the theology of evangelism—finding and folding the lost and multiplying congregations of the redeemed. This is an essential part of all true theology. The many passages of Scripture commanding effective evangelism require the formation of explicit doctrines along these lines.

The second course would teach how to train laymen and laywomen for evangelism. Lay people, if trained in evangelism, are most effective communicators. They reach their fellow workers, fellow faculty members, fellow employers and employees. Lay people must be trained in effective evangelism.

The third course would teach how to multiply congregations in North American Anglo and minority populations. Each of the multitudinous segments of American society is a distinct population, in which Christian congregations must be multiplied. The gospel must be stated in one way to win highly educated secularists and in other ways to win recent immigrants who speak English very imperfectly.

A fourth course would accurately describe the state of the churches and denominations in other continents. Do they comprise 1 percent or 90 percent of the population? Are they growing or declining? Are they carrying on effective evangelism or merely looking after themselves? How can they be helped to become evangelistically more powerful? Are they sending missionaries to their own unreached populations, or must this be done by missionaries from other nation-states? Are they working to produce a more Christian social order?

The fifth course would deal with the ways of evangelism that God was most greatly blessing to the redemption of women and men. The ways of evangelism differ for various populations. Those which are effective in university populations will yield no results among the illiterate tribesmen in the heart of Africa. Those which multiply congregations among blue-collar workers will not be effective among white-collar people. Those effective in west London are singularly ineffective in east London, where 98 percent of the English remain out of the church. Because the ways of effective evangelism are so numerous and vary from population to population and from age to age, this fifth course may run for two semesters.

Would five or six four-hour courses on evangelism be pleasing to God? Would not such a program enormously advantage the existing church? Would this not very speedily make for a much better and more moral and just world? If the answers to these three questions are yes, then why should not every school of theological education require five four-hour courses on effective evangelism—i.e., church growth?

Objections to These Proposals Are Certain to Be Voiced

Let me deal at once with one possible objection—that all the existing subjects also need to be taught. Which of them can be compressed? Will church history or Old Testament, New Testament, systematic theology, Christian education, or worship give up part of its courses? Quite impossible.

The effective answer to this objection is that as new situations develop, new courses of the curriculum have been made available and always will be. The curriculum formed between 1550 and 1950 is not the best curriculum for a tremendously changed world. As God's will for the present world is made clear and becomes feasible, all good Christians will seek to bring their individual and corporate lives into harmony with it. In order to make churches and denominations more obedient to Christ's command to *matheteusate panta ta ethne,* "disciple all peoples," a command now being perceived in a new way, seminary faculties and their boards of trustees will beyond question, bit by bit, reorganize their curricula.

To be sure, some seminaries will not. Other seminaries will. Those seminaries which will not will observe their congregations and denominations shrink. Those which make the changes will observe their congregations and denominations grow.

It is worth remembering that in the past the most orthodox and sound theological seminaries have often been those of very slow growing denominations. In a nation whose population has been exploding, into which large numbers of immigrants have poured, the denominations whose seminaries have been committed to teaching only those portions of theology which people already converted needed to know have often been the least growing.

At the same time the Pentecostals during the past eighty years have grown enormously even though their seminaries and Bible colleges have not been ranked high by the prestigious seminaries of the world.

Every theological seminary must decide whether the ideal denomination, most pleasing to God, would be one that cares only for existing Christians or one that, in true New Testament fashion, both cares for existing Christians and multiplies churches in unreached portions of humanity. If the answer is that the church most pleasing to God is one that in every possible way seeks to disciple *panta ta ethne* as well as care for existing Christians, then the seminary curriculum must prepare ministers to do both tasks.

Every seminary has a course on homiletics, the effective presentation of the gospel. At first thought, effective courses on homiletics are all that is needed. Unfortunately, homiletics is usually held to be the presentation of the gospel in sermon form to those who attend church. These, with few exceptions, are not the unsaved but the saved, the practicing Christians, the existing congregation. As the thoughtful minister prepares a message for these, he inevitably stresses what they, the saved, need to know. He talks about how Christians can become better Christians. He assumes that those listening to him are already followers of the Lord Jesus. He frames his sermon in language and thought forms that will appeal to the segment of society to which his flock belongs and from which his salary comes. All this is excellent. The pastor must indeed care for the flock. He must indeed preach convincing, well-thought-out, and persuasive sermons. But such sermons do not reach the very large percentage of the population that attends no church.

Here in the United States there are possibly only 50 million practicing Christians regularly in church on Sunday. A hundred million nominal Christians also are to be found in church now and then, particularly at Christmas and Easter. Finally there are 80-90 million who never darken the doors of any church. Professors of homiletics may be assured that the sermons their students preach will certainly reach and influence the 50 million. They will be heard now and then by a scattering of men and women in the 100 million. But they will never be heard by the 90 million. As we explore the subject of theological education and church growth, we must therefore ask, Must not any Bible college or seminary that would seek to obey God in the next thirty years here in America teach ways in which all congregations, all denominations, and all ministers will use a significant portion of their time in finding and folding the 180 million lost sheep in the United States?

It cannot be said too emphatically that too many seminaries in all six continents are preparing ministers who are engaged solely in looking after—maintaining—the current congregations. Just how they do this will vary from situation to situation, congregation to congregation, and denomination to denomination. Far too many congregations and denominations, facing the most responsive world ever to exist, are spending 85-99 percent of their time, prayer, money, and thought in looking after themselves.

On October 11, 1985, I received a letter from a very able seminary graduate who has served as a pastor of two local churches and now occupies a position in a theological seminary in India. That seminary is planning to send him to the United States for further study, preparing him to become a professor of church history in the seminary. Concerning the churches of several denominations in a densely populated part of India, he writes the following:

> I believe that reaching the receptive Ezhavas is a responsibility of the churches in that area. These churches have to be mission minded, to win the receptive peoples of the population. The government of India will not give visas to missionaries. What-

ever is done must be done by the churches. Unfortunately, the churches, instead of being mission minded have become institution minded, with scores of schools, hospitals, and nowadays so-called development work. . . . Our churches have lots of money, but they spend it on other things than winning non-Christians to Christ. The root cause of this is that our pastors and leaders do not preach and teach about discipling all the castes. Also none of the pastors is trained in effective evangelism. That is why I want to study missions. The seminary is prepared to send me to the United States to study church history. I have a hard time to decide between my own convictions that I need to study how to win non-Christians and the seminary's desire to have me specialize in church history.

This letter might have been written from ten thousand mission fields and from any one of hundreds of seminaries. Seminaries believe that they are training ministers, not evangelists. Seminaries believe that the main task of the minister is to be doctrinally and historically correct. Seminaries are not missionary societies, they emphasize. As a result, in the midst of a most responsive world too many denominations grow very slowly. Sometimes the most orthodox, Reformed, and doctrinally sound denominations are also the least growing. It is also true that often the most modern, advanced, and wide-awake denominations are slow growing.

As I discuss these matters with Christian leaders of today, they frequently reply, "Yes, of course, such courses must be in schools of evangelism or missions. We quite agree that the unreached must hear the gospel rapidly and effectively. But the theological seminary is not the place in which to teach such courses. If the church wants these taught (and we hope it does), the church must establish separate institutions to deal with these important topics." What shall we say to these objections?

The Theological Institution Has Two Essential Tasks
The fundamental—repeat, *fundamental*—task of every minister must be seen as *both* caring for the flock and finding and folding the lost—including, alas, vast numbers of very nominal "Christians."

No true shepherd will ever say, "Only such sheep as care to follow me will I shepherd." The true shepherd constantly seeks for the uncared for, the lost, the hungry, and the wandering sheep. The Lord Jesus said the true shepherd leaves the ninety-nine in the fold and goes out to seek the one lost sheep. Today's shepherds may have twenty in the fold and eighty lost in the wilderness in danger from wolves and lions. All true followers of the Lord Jesus must share and incorporate in their own lives His overpowering concern that unbelievers in vast numbers become believers, that they repent, be baptized, and become living members of His body.

Since the seminary is preparing candidates to become pastors—effective shepherds—in a largely secular, humanistic, and indeed pagan world, the seminary should change the curriculum that was formed many years ago to fit a "Christian world" that no longer exists. Seminaries should prepare ministers both to help existing Christians to become better Christians and to lead multitudes of secularists, humanists, followers of the religion of scientism, Hinduists and on and on to becoming believing, trusting, and obedient followers of Christ.

What the seminary teaches in regard to carrying out eternal God's command to proclaim the gospel to *panta ta ethne*, leading them to faith and obedience, must constantly be measured. It must be measured against the degree to which seminary graduates are effective in leading unbelievers, agnostics, materialists, Muslims, Jews, and other non-Christians to Christian faith. It must be measured against multiplying new congregations. Seminary courses in effective evangelism must be counted good not merely if they are academically impeccable but if those who take such courses become good harvesters, bringing in many sheaves from the ripened fields. The ultimate test as to whether seminary graduates make good pastors has too frequently been whether such a pastor cared for existing flocks. Certainly existing flocks must be cared for; about that there can be no doubt. However, in a nation rapidly becoming humanist, secularist, and materialist, the ultimate test must also be how well the pastor and his people win unbelievers to Christian faith and multiply new congregations. Every congregation should plant and mother a new congregation every two years. No congregation should remain barren and childless. Only as a vast passion to be "all things to all men *in order to win some*" seizes congregations, denominations, and seminaries can God's will for the world be truly carried out.

There can be no doubt that eternal God desires that men and women in all *ethne* (segments of society) believe on Jesus Christ and become living, obedient members of His body, the church. Since at this point there will be no debate in any Christian audience, in the following chapters we shall ask how theological schools, congregations, and denominations can carry out much more effective evangelism. We shall look at the world as it is. We shall see the unsaved three-quarters of earth's population. We shall examine the various ways in which different vast populations divided into tens of thousands of *ethne* can be led to saving faith in Christ. We shall discuss how the theological seminary not only in America but around the world can become a more effective instrument in God's hands. We shall present many ways in which seminary graduates can find and bring home God's lost children.

There are no doubt other ways to multiply Christian congregations in the tremendously complex mosaic of humankind. Nevertheless, I trust that these thoughts will prove stimulating and will be one small addition to the surging river of thought dealing with how Christians should meet their present opportunities—how seminaries and Bible schools should prepare their students, who are the most important segment of society in the world today.

As we look upon the white harvest fields stretched away in so many directions, we must indeed pray the Lord to send men and women into the fields who will know how to reap and how to bring back multitudes of sheaves to the Master's barn.

2

God Commands
Church Growth

Look on Fields White to Harvest

As the Lord Jesus, accompanied by His disciples, walked through Samaria, He said earnestly to them, "Open your eyes and look at the fields! They are ripe for harvest. Even now the reaper draws his wages, even now he harvests the crop for eternal life, so that the sower and the reaper may be glad together" (John 4:35-36). The Lord also said, "The harvest is plentiful but the workers are few. Ask the Lord of the harvest, therefore, to send out workers into his harvest field" (Matt. 9:37-38).

His disciples had thought that the actual harvest of souls, the actual multiplication of Christ's followers, would come in some future time—"after four months." Our Lord, knowing what they were thinking, said most clearly, No, not at some future time but now. The fields are white to harvest. If you wait, the ripened grain will fall to the ground and rot. Ripe fields must be reaped now. These sheaves must be carried into the master's barn now. Bringing in one sheaf every ten days is not what God wants. He wants a sheaf every two minutes. Pray, therefore, for the Lord of harvest to send laborers—many laborers—into His harvest.

This was the situation even before His followers had rightly understood the Christian message, even before the Holy Spirit had descended upon them, even before the Lord Jesus had become the sacrifice for sins. These words of our Lord are more applicable today in New York, Los Angeles, and all other cities around the world than they were there in Samaria nearly two thousand years ago. They are not only applicable; they should be understood as a command to reap all ripe urban and rural fields now.

When we disobey this command, we disobey our Lord. He said, "Look on the ripe fields." We look elsewhere, maintaining that there are many other tasks, such as caring for the existing flock, training future ministers, and working for brotherhood and justice, that are much more important than bringing in sheaves of ripened grain. This passage is not often thought of as a command to evangelize effectively, bringing multitudes of reborn men and women into a living relationship with the Triune God. Christians today in many branches of the church are doing many good things, but alas, too few of them are girding themselves with sickles and ropes and bringing in a sheaf every two minutes. This is a significant crisis facing today's church and all its seminaries.

The New Testament is full of passages that indicate the steady purpose of the Triune God to make the gospel known throughout the entire world and to institute a new kind of life based on complete obedience to Him, a complete surrender of self to Christ, and a mighty multiplication of Christian congregations.

Eternal God's Command

For example, Paul writes to the Romans, "Through him and for his name's sake, we received grace and apostleship to call people from among all the Gentiles to the obedience that comes from faith" (1:5).The whole epistle, which has so frequently been treated as a summary of essential Christian doctrines, contains an essential doctrine frequently overlooked. Paul in 1:5 says that he has been ordained of God "to call people from among all the Gentiles to the obedience that comes from faith." The Greek phrase for Gentiles is *ta ethne*—the peoples, the tribes, castes, segments of society, urbanites and ruralites. Paul declares that he has been commissioned by God to call all the peoples of the world to the obedience that comes from faith. That is God's command. Doing that is essential Christian conduct. No one can be a good Christian who does not engage in this enterprise. God intends that all men shall have the opportunity to accept Jesus Christ as God and Savior. The only way that this can happen is for Christians everywhere to consider the proclamation of the gospel, the winning of men and women to

Christ, and the multiplication of living churches as God's command.

Not only does the epistle to the Romans begin in this fashion; it also ends by stressing church growth. Look at 16:25-27:

> Now to him who is able to establish you by my gospel and the proclamation of Jesus Christ, according to the revelation of the mystery hidden for long ages past, but now revealed and made known through the prophetic writings by the command of the eternal God, so that all [*ethne*] might believe and obey him—to the only wise God be glory forever through Jesus Christ! Amen.

This is a magnificent ascription of praise to God. It ends with the words, "to the only wise God be glory forever through Jesus Christ! Amen." Paul in this wonderful passage piles word on word and phrase on phrase until the whole gleams and shines in the sunlight. However, if we go back and read the passage carefully, we shall find a most effective command to evangelize the whole world. I lay before you the exact quotation. I shall leave out some qualifying words and phrases. "My gospel . . . hidden for long ages past, . . . but now revealed . . . by the command of the eternal God, so that [*panta ta ethne*] might believe and obey him."

This closing passage unquestionably indicates that eternal God Himself has commanded that the gospel be made known to *panta ta ethne*, leading them to "believe and obey Him." Wherever Paul went, urged on by this command of eternal God, he proclaimed the gospel, won men and women to Christ, and multiplied churches. His letters almost always went to churches, not individuals. In Philippi he won not only Lydia, that seller of purple, but the jailer and his family and many others. He did not write to Lydia or the jailer. He wrote to "all the saints in Christ Jesus at Philippi, together with the overseers and deacons," i.e., the whole congregation (Phil. 1:1).

Eternal God's command voiced in Romans 16:25-26 echoes what Paul wrote in Romans 1:5 and is a most essential part of the entire epistle. Indeed, it may be considered the driving force behind the epistle. Paul's life was lived in obedience to this command. Eternal God Himself commands that the gospel be made known to all the peoples of earth. Since it is impossible to imagine that eternal God commanded this to Paul only and to no other Christian, we are forced to the conclusion that eternal God sent His Son, the Word made flesh, precisely so that *panta ta ethne*, all the peoples of the world, should be led to believe and obey Him, and thus be saved. God wants His lost children found and lays this command firmly on His redeemed in all times in all places.

While Paul does not say to the Romans, "You as individuals and as congregations must engage in world evangelization," surely such a message is implied in these two and other passages in the book of Romans. All Christians march under this command. What they do will, of course, depend very greatly upon the circumstances in which they find themselves. But that command which energized the lives of the apostles must also energize the lives of all Christians and certainly all students and professors in schools engaged in theological education throughout the world.

It is certainly natural that Christians in all places and all ages should think of proclaiming the gospel to *panta ta ethne* as something beyond their own capacities. Nevertheless, all great revivals of the church have rested on first one man and then many, *hearing and then obeying this command*. In the days of William Carey very few, if any, Christians in the British Isles thought of world evangelization as commanded by God. Then William Carey heard this command. When he voiced his convictions that God was commanding His church to proclaim the gospel to all peoples, he was sharply rebuked. A noted leader of his communion turned to him in an open meeting and said, "Sit down, young man. When it pleases God to evangelize the heathen, He will do it without your aid or mine. Sit down."

Fortunately, William Carey obeyed God rather than this misguided elder, and the entire history of the world began to change.

Eternal God's command so clearly voiced in the passage we have considered must today be heard and obeyed. The process may well start with divinity schools where the future leaders of the Christian cause are trained. As seminaries, individual Christians, congregations, and other Christian organizations hear this command, they will turn their attention to the enormous fields white to harvest—the great urbanizations rising in every land, the thousands of unreached peoples from among whom very few, if any, have become Christian, and the increasing millions of secularists, materialists, agnostics, and atheists.

The Ultimate Authority Commands Worldwide Discipling

Then Jesus came to them and said, "All authority in heaven and on earth has been given to me. Therefore go and make disciples of all nations, baptizing them in the name of the Father and of the Son and of the Holy Spirit" (Matt. 28:18-19).

How striking it is that the New Testament records that not only does eternal God command world evangelization, but the risen and reigning Lord does also. He says, "All authority in heaven and on earth has been given to me." What overwhelming authority! What He is about to say does not come from the carpenter of Nazareth or from the itinerant preacher, going up and down Palestine not knowing where he was going to sleep that night. It does not come even from the One dying on Calvary as an atonement for sins. It comes from Him to whom all authority in heaven and on earth has been given, the risen Lord.

What is this ultimate Authority going to say? Is He going to say, "Love the Lord your God and your neighbor as yourself"? That certainly is an important command, but He doesn't say it here. Is He going to say, "Go to church and worship God"? That also is important, but it is not what He says. What He does say is, "Therefore *matheteusate panta ta ethne." Matheteusate* is a verb in the imperative. It means enroll in my school or enlist in my army or incorporate in my body. *Panta* means all, and *ta ethne* means the peoples, the tribes, the castes, the segments of society everywhere. All are to be discipled.

When the Bible was translated into English by order of King James I, the missionary concern of the Protestants in northern Europe was minimal, or more accurately, nonexistent. Consequently, they translated this passage as "Go ye therefore, and teach all nations." The more accurate translation is "Disciple all the peoples, all segments of society everywhere." The ultimate Authority in the universe commands this; it is clearly incumbent on all Christians to obey it.

This was the command that motivated the Student Volunteer

Movement. John Mott, Robert Speer, and Robert Wilder, hearing this command, framed the battle cry of the Student Volunteer Movement as "the evangelization of the world in this generation." The Student Volunteer Movement has faded; but the command still rings out clear and unequivocal. It should be taught by all theological seminaries, divinity schools, and Bible colleges to all ministers in training.

Liberal Christians in the past half century have consistently denigrated this command. Some have maintained that it was never spoken by the risen Lord but was added by an editor, perhaps as late as A.D. 110. However, all those who believe that the Bible is the inspired, authoritative, true, and utterly dependable Word of God still hear it as our Lord spoke it—disciple all the peoples of planet earth. This command sends them to multiply churches in the towns and cities where they live and among the unreached billions in the whole earth. It is important to realize that the Lord Jesus is not here giving a suggestion to His followers. He is not making a recommendation. He is not saying, "Do this if you find time or if it is financially feasible." He is not saying to divinity schools, "Please squeeze this in as an elective." He is issuing a command—disciple all the peoples of earth.

This task today is largely undone. Not only are there more than 100 million people in the United States who have yet to be won to ardent Christian faith, but there are 4 billion unwon in the world, and by the year 2000 there will be at least 5 billion. Unless Christians listen to and obey this command, they cannot be fully Christian. One has only to listen to the television broadcasts to realize that we do not live in a "Christian America"; we live in a secular, materialistic, indeed an almost pagan America in which practicing Christians are a minority. True, at present we are an influential minority, but unless we obey this command at home and abroad, we may soon become a much smaller and less influential minority.

On this point we would do well to listen to the Rev. Mark Christensen of the Missouri Synod Lutheran Church. He says that it is becoming increasingly clear that an enormous shift toward a secular culture is taking place in America today. He sees an urgent need to relate to the unchurched in a manner and method that makes sense to them.

Kevin Perrotta, a Roman Catholic who lives in Ann Arbor, Michigan, writes:

> The integrity of Christian belief, life, and mission is at stake in the contemporary conflict between the gospel and secular culture. . . . Our own time is marked by widespread rejection of historic Christian beliefs. . . . The deep anti-Christian trends of our time [must be combated by all Christians].[1]

Both these men describe the society in which the church now lives in a way that makes it absolutely urgent for all schools of theology to devote considerable time to teaching an evangelism that will prove effective in an increasingly secular and materialistic civilization. There is no time to lose. Seminaries and Bible colleges must act now.

The Apostle Paul Commands Winning as Many Unbelievers as Possible

The fourth command to which I would direct the attention of theological seminaries and ministers and all practicing Christians is found in 1 Corinthians. It reads as follows: "I try to please all men in everything I do . . . that they may be saved. *Be imitators of me* as I am of Christ" (1 Cor. 10:33–11:1, RSV, italics added).

First Corinthians 9 and 10 is usually thought of as Paul's comments on eating meat offered to idols, and, of course, he is talking about that. However, what guides the entire thought of these two chapters is the conviction that all Christians should be all things to all men, *in order to win some.* Paul says this has been the guiding principle of his life, and then he commands all Christians to imitate him in this respect as he imitates Christ. He says very clearly, whatever the circumstances in which you find yourself, even that of eating meat in a friend's house, make yourself a Christian witness; do not raise unnecessary difficulties. Do not assume that your jailer is your enemy. Address him as your friend. Do not believe that only as a free man can you preach the gospel. Believe, rather, that when

---

1. Personal letter to Donald McGavran January 10, 1986, from Kevin Perrotta, Associate Director of the Center for Pastoral Renewal, Ann Arbor, Mich.

you preach it with chains on your hands and feet, it is more effective than when you are free.

This is not only Paul's way of life but one that all Christians, especially theological seminaries, should practice. It is at this point with a command voiced in this fashion that the science of missiology today speaks most relevantly to all Christians. The science of world evangelization (which is what missiology is) says clearly: If you are to be understood, you must speak the language of your listener. You must know his culture and speak from within it. You must voice the message so that it will make sense to him. You must not sound like a Jew trying to make others into Jews or like an American trying to bring others to American culture and scientific achievement. *No!* You must be all things to all men *in order to win some.*

To the urbanite masses in Mexico City you must speak from within their culture, saying to them in effect, God has prepared a way of salvation for you, living at your level, suffering your disabilities, surrounded by your temptations, anticipating the rewards you anticipate. Begin walking in the way God has prepared for you. Believe on the Lord Jesus Christ; live as saved men and women. Whether you live free or with chains on your hands and feet makes little difference; live redeemed lives wherever you are.

To be sure, implicit in the gospel is the assurance that as *ethnos* after *ethnos* is discipled, as society after society is Christianized, tremendous advances in justice, brotherhood, peace, and good living will be practicable and will be achieved. If we want human improvement, nothing we can do will secure it as rapidly and as effectively as discipling *panta ta ethne*. The colossal error of some misguided Christians is to believe that we can have a just and egalitarian society without men and women becoming believing Christians. The Bible gives no grounds for any such hope. Nor, for that matter, does human history. Clear-eyed vision indicates that until men and women are reborn, no great moral advance is likely to occur.

Many Biblical Passages Confirm God's Command
As we consider the overwhelming purpose of the New Testament

to evangelize the entire world, we remember the many passages in which our Lord assumes that these express commands will be obeyed. I refer to three. The first is when our Lord was in Bethany at the home of Simon, and a woman brought an alabaster jar of expensive perfume and poured it on His head. When His disciples objected to this waste of money, He reproved them saying, "Wherever the gospel is preached throughout the world, what she has done will also be told, in memory of her" (Mark 14:9). Our Lord assumed that eternal God's command would be carried out, that all schools of theological education would teach effective evangelism responsibly, and the gospel would be proclaimed *in all the world.* There are many such passages.

The second important example is found in Matthew 11:28-30, where our Lord said, "Come to me, all you who are weary and burdened, and I will give you rest. Take my yoke upon you and learn from me, for I am gentle and humble in heart, and you will find rest for your souls. For my yoke is easy and my burden is light." He certainly was not speaking only to those who were weary and burdened in the few dozens or hundreds who were then listening to Him. He was voicing His permanent, perpetual, worldwide invitation, to all those of all cultures in all countries and all ages who are weary and burdened. The Christian faith assumes that it is the only true and full understanding of God's plan for the entire human race.

This is especially important in America today, where a brotherly attitude toward all nationalities and minorities is held to be politically necessary. The science of anthropology frequently assures us that all cultures are equal. This makes it easy to assume that all religions also voice essential truths. Some are possibly more exact than others, but all religions are good for their adherents to follow. In reaction to the imperial era when Europe ruled most of the rest of the world, democratic America is saying loud and clear, Your own ways—and religions—are probably the very best ways for you.

Christians must think much more exactly. While appreciating the good in other cultures, Christians must hear Christ's invitation to all those in all cultures and all religions who are weary and burdened to come to Him, obey Him, and find rest.

The Old Testament also has many passages that affirm that God the Father almighty, Maker of heaven and earth, from the very beginning intended all people to leave their idols and follow Him. Let me mention just one passage. In Genesis 12:3 God says to Abram, "In you all the families of the earth shall be blessed." God wills the salvation of *panta ta ethne*, all the peoples in every continent. God commands their evangelization.

Theological Educators and Christians
Must Obey These Imperatives

God's command to His church to evangelize the world must be heard and carried out by all components of the church. World evangelization must not be limited to missionary societies and professional evangelists. These commands are laid upon every Christian. "Imitate me" was not written to Paul's fellow evangelists. It was written to the Christian fellowship in Corinth, to all its members, men and women alike. The entire body of Christ needs to hear and obey the imperative to world evangelization. An effective spread of the gospel should become a substantial part of every seminary's curriculum. Only then will it become a part of family prayers in every Christian home.

This is of particular importance in schools of theological education. It is a part of a true and adequate theology. Any knowledge of God, the true and ever-living God, must give priority to His commands that all His lost children be found. They must be found in all segments of society—the rich, the poor, the rural, the urban, the literate, the illiterate, Americans, Africans, Asians, and Europeans—all the lost sheep are dear to God's heart and must be brought to belief.

The words *panta ta ethne*, so often used, must not be overlooked in divinity schools and Bible colleges. God clearly intends that all segments of society in all nations of the world not only hear the gospel but obey the gospel and become followers of the Lord. Some, maybe many, will hear and reject the gospel. That is of their own choosing. God does not circumvent their wills. But He does want the Christianization of all segments of society. It is the high duty of the church to work at this enormous task. In this book this truth will be constantly held in mind. It is from this perspective that we will view current society, world history, and the duties and responsibilities of all arms of the church and especially of schools of theological education, both faculty and students.

3

The Urgency of
Church Growth in America

The urgency of church growth in America today is highlighted by the fact that during the years 1965–75 ten of the largest branches of the church not only were static but actually declined. One declined by 32 percent. Another notable denomination declined by 19 percent. The three united churches declined 12 percent, 11 percent, and 10 percent. Five others declined 7 percent, 6 percent, 6 percent, 5 percent, and 2 percent.

All this took place in a free country. No church was being persecuted. Seminaries were never freer. National prosperity was at an all-time high. The country as a whole was regarded as the most powerful nation in the world. Its institutions of learning attracted students from every nation on earth. The awesome power of the atom had been harnessed. Thermonuclear plants were turning out enormous quantities of electricity. Public health stood at an all-time high. Men and women were living longer lives. The rate of infant mortality had sharply declined. The battle for brotherhood was being won. Blacks were being treated more and more as fellow citizens rather than as members of an inferior race.

Yet in this great country many branches of the church were static or even declining. Seminaries, with few exceptions, offered required courses in everything except evangelism. Often the most orthodox churches were the least growing. While their rock-hard theological convictions were correct and clearly based upon the Bible, their members were not taught how to come out of ripe fields bearing many sheaves. This was especially true of liberal denominations. In fact, the largest liberal denominations were declining. Too often church members of both liberal and orthodox denominations, led by well-trained pastors, sat down in some far corner of a ripe field

24

under a shady tree to sing praises to God, voice biblically correct doctrines, and pray.

As He always does, God had abundantly blessed those who were His devoted followers. They had become more prosperous, more respected, and more honored. The gulf between them and the unsaved widened. Their prosperity had made growth difficult.

Let me illustrate this important point. In the mid-sixties I was conducting the annual church growth seminar in Winona Lake, Indiana. Winona Lake is the national headquarters of the Free Methodist Church. One evening six bishops of the Free Methodist Church took me out to dinner in order to discuss with me a problem that was greatly concerning them. In northern Indiana, northwest Ohio, and southeastern Michigan their denomination was strong. They had many Free Methodist congregations. The Free Methodists were an honored and respected part of many communities. Yet they were not growing. Why?

Into that section of North America during the preceding thirty years had come large numbers of Appalachians. These Appalachians, who were all whites, were less educated, less prosperous, and less respected than the members of the Free Methodist congregations.

"How does it happen," asked the bishops, "that when we try to win the Appalachians to Christ and membership in our churches, they may come to our churches once or twice, but they do not come back again? If occasionally some one of them joins a Free Methodist Church, he or she continues as a member for only a few months. What must we do to win large numbers of this segment of the population?"

As we discussed the situation, the picture became clear. The Appalachians were a different stratum in the population. They did not feel at home in congregations made up of prosperous, respected, and well-educated women and men. They frequently walked to church smoking cigarettes. They did not feel at home in devoutly Christian, highly respectable, and prosperous congregations. Consequently, the Free Methodists were unable to win many from this large unchurched segment of the population. This was not the only reason for lack of growth, but it certainly was one.

Let me give you another illustration from my own denomination.

While I was home on furlough in 1940, the United Christian Missionary Society sent me to speak on missions to a hundred-year-old congregation of the Christian churches located in northeast Ohio, about seven miles from the heart of a great growing city. The congregation had been made up of prosperous farmers. It had a fine church building, which seated perhaps a hundred people. Its pastor said to me, "The city is growing out all around us. Farmers sell farms, which are then subdivided into lots and sold to city people. But so far we have been unable to win these people to our church. They think of us as a country church." Consequently, the church continued as a nongrowing rural congregation on the edge of a growing city.

Eight years later, in 1948, I was again on furlough and was sent on deputation to this same congregation. The Sunday I spoke there the church was filled to overflowing. People stood on the verandah looking in through the open windows. Chairs filled the central aisle. The space in front of the pulpit was less than two feet wide. I said to the pastor, "What on earth happened?"

He replied, "For many years we were unable to win the city population. They might come a time or two, but they did not return. Practically none of them put in their membership here. Then we had a month-long evangelistic campaign. We asked all who attended to help us found a new vigorous suburban church of Christ-honoring, Bible-believing men and women. As a result 114 persons, including many whole families, declared that they wished to become members of the church. The church board composed of the old farming families resigned, and we held new elections. We elected new elders, deacons, and Sunday school teachers, many of them from among the new people."

"The old guard must have been very grieved and indignant," I said.

"No," he replied, "they were delighted. This is what they had wanted to happen but did not know how to bring it about. The city population now felt that they were not joining a church governed by a board of elderly farmers. They were now joining a church of their own kind of people. It made all the difference in the world."

Too frequently opportunities for church growth lie all around existing congregations, but these opportunities are not bought up. Consequently, whole segments of the population remain undiscipled. Vast amounts of ripe grain fall to the ground and rot. This ought to be a matter of great concern to theological educators and other leaders of the church.

On the Sunday before Labor Day, 1985, in southern California the newspapers reported that two and a half million people went to the beaches to spend the day frolicking on the sand. The number of people in church that day was considerably less than half a million.

If eternal God's command is to be carried out, if *panta ta ethne,* all the segments of society in North America, are to be discipled, we must find ways to multiply living congregations in every segment. Existing congregations must not assume that they are the only churches and that other people have to join them. As the New Testament so clearly indicates, it is God's will that the Christian faith flow into every segment of the population everywhere.

Unless we dig channels for such a flow, we shall continue to see many denominations—both mainline and evangelical—become static or even decline. The 1965–75 record, alas, can easily be duplicated and, indeed, is being duplicated in too many cases today.

Does Doctrinal Correctness
Frequently Coincide With Decline?

I fear that too often doctrinal correctness does coincide with decline. This tremendously emphasizes the urgency of church growth in North America today. In a land where we could multiply Christian congregations and Christian convictions enormously we are too often standing still. I consider doctrinal correctness of the highest importance. The church of Jesus Christ must not be—indeed, cannot be—a heretical church. What the Bible clearly teaches must be what the church teaches.

Nevertheless, we must all recognize that doctrinal correctness frequently coincides with prosperity, respectability, higher education—and nongrowth. Doctrinally correct denominations tend to become so different that they do not attract people of the general citizenry.

There are three reasons for this. The first is that a given denomination may stress only certain doctrines. It may insist, for example, that all Christians avoid worldly vices or become well versed in the doctrines of grace or strive for social justice. And each of these is good and correct as far as it goes. But a denomination may at the same time stop short of teaching doctrines that demand effective evangelism.

The second reason for failure to grow is that God does unquestionably bless those who obey Him and live according to His commands. This blessing too often and unnecessarily isolates them from the unsaved multitudes. As doctrinally correct congregations and denominations are blessed by God, their members become better citizens, husbands, wives, sons, and daughters than those who are servants of Satan or who live according to the dictates of their own hearts. The doctrinally correct must continually work to make sure that the blessings they receive do not shut them off from the unsaved multitudes. God's lost children must have ready access to them and must feel welcome in their presence. Evangelicals in particular here in North America must make sure that the honesty, kindness, compassion, and love that their lives demonstrate do not insulate them from the great bulk of the population. Being saved and being good practicing Christians must also mean being especially concerned neighbors, especially open women and men. Only so will they be able to communicate the gospel.

A third and most important reason for failure to grow is that unfortunately the best of Christians frequently never hear God's command to disciple all the segments of humankind. They do not bring sheaves out of ripe fields. They do not proclaim the gospel to all peoples, leading them to the obedience of faith. They do not even try to *matheteusate panta ta ethne*. They leave these good activities to missionaries and evangelists. Too frequently ministers believe that their chief duty is looking after the existing congregations, preaching good sermons, and counseling those who come to them.

As a result, correctness in regard to only some doctrines frequently does coincide with decline or at least with a static condition. The correctness of which I have just spoken is frequently correctness in regard to aspects of Christian faith that do not explicitly require a gathering of the sheaves.

A historical reason for this strange and distressing neglect of discipling all peoples is that when the Protestant faith was being firmly established in northern Europe, access to the rest of the world was cut off by the Portuguese and Spanish navies in the Atlantic and the Muslim armies in the East and South. Consequently, all great leaders of the church taught that the Great Commission was given to the apostles only and expired after their death.

Let me assure you that full doctrinal correctness will certainly lead to effective evangelism. It must, however, be correctness in regard to *all* doctrines. We cannot omit the doctrines commanding that the body of Christ and all its separate parts continuously engage in finding lost sons and daughters and bringing them back to the Father's house. This view of essential Christian conduct and essential Christian obedience is, to be sure, implied in many doctrines. For example, the doctrine of the atonement is not limited to existing Christians. It does not state that Christ died to save only members of the existing churches. If it is correctly understood as atonement for those who believe, age after age, among all people everywhere, then the doctrine of the atonement itself impels us toward effective evangelization. The same is true of many other doctrines.

Consequently, we must say that true *and complete* doctrinal correctness will promote church growth. However, the very common incomplete doctrinal correctness taught by so many Bible colleges and seminaries unfortunately does create static congregations and denominations.

The Tidal Wave of Secularism, Materialism, and Paganism

We must now mention again the tidal wave of secularism, materialism, and agnosticism or atheism that has spread across Europe and North America.

Anyone who regards the reading material—books, magazines, newspapers, and the like—and the radio and television programs of North American peoples must be impressed with the agnostic, materialistic, and indeed atheistic teaching of many of these books and programs. Most university professors are unbelievers. Their teachings, the books they write, and the lectures they give strongly influence their students to become like them. Many young women and men, decidedly Christian until they go to college, waver in their faith as they study under these professors. They enter college or university practicing Christians. They leave university either very nominal Christians or not Christians at all.

Many reasons cause this tidal wave of secularism. Among the more important are the following, stated here from a non-Christian point of view.

> First, since we live in one world and ought to live in friendship and amity with all peoples everywhere, we must accept their cultures and their religion as equal to our own. We must not try to convert them. We may dialogue with them, but we certainly should not evangelize them. There is truth in all religions. Adherents of each religion tend to think that their own is more truthful and realistic than others. If we are to live amicably with all peoples on earth, we must hold their religions to be as good for them as our religion is for us.

> The second reason for this tidal wave of secularism is that many anthropologists and historians believe that man evolved from monkeys exactly as present-day whales evolved from warm-blooded animals that played along the edges of the ocean a hundred million years ago. God did not create man in His own image. Strictly by genetic accident more and more intelligent apes were born, began to walk on two feet, grew larger brains, began to use weapons, and finally evolved into man. No God was necessary for all this. The student is asked to choose between the idea that God created man out of mud and the much more reasonable belief that man evolved from monkeys.

It is in this secularized society that the Christian faith must spread. *Bible colleges and seminaries in particular must frame, put into operation, test, and refine methods of evangelism that God blesses to bring secularists and humanists to Christian faith.* Theological seminaries must teach men and women how to win convinced secularists to ardent Christian faith. Unless we speak to this growing component of modern society, we shall not bring many sheaves out of the secularistic, humanistic modern populations.

A False View of the Bible

A major reason for today's vast indifference to church growth, i.e., to effective evangelism, is a prevalent low view of the Bible. Under the influence of European rationalism, biblical scholars started more than a hundred years ago to analyze the various books of the Bible. For example, in the book of Genesis certain passages were believed to be written by Jehovah worshipers, others by the worshipers of Elohim, still others by the writers of Deuteronomy, and still others by members of a priestly school. Thus a biblical scholar would distinguish passages in Genesis according to four different sources—J, E, D, and P. From this beginning, endless speculations arose as to which were the more authentic and true passages. This process, repeated in book after book of the Bible, destroyed any notion of real authority. In denominations where this view generally prevailed, the church lost its power. The Bible was not the Word of God inspired, authoritative, and utterly reliable. It was a very human document. In it, no doubt, were many excellent teachings, and it was the duty of Christians to pick out those teachings most applicable to today and to disregard the rest.

Wherever Christians have come to hold a low opinion of the Bible—whether that described above or any other—eternal God's command to proclaim the gospel to *panta ta ethne*, leading them to obedience of faith, is greatly damaged, if not destroyed.

However, where a high view of the Bible obtains, where it is held to be the inspired and utterly dependable Word of God, the ultimate authority for human life, the only infallible rule of faith and practice, God's Word to all people—there tremendous concern for the unsaved, for those who do not live according to God's Word, is certain to mark the true church. There the urgency of winning the lost will be felt by seminary professors, ministers, and lay people alike. There the church will come alive.

Conclusion

Ripe harvest fields are often not being reaped—or even seen—in North America. Students and faculties in theological institutions need to face frankly the fact that too frequently Christian denominations—even evangelical denominations—are growing very slowly. Alas, in some cases they have become static or are actually declining. Not only must theological students and their teachers themselves carry out God's commands, but all pastors must train church members to do the same. Ripe harvest fields—whether of secularists or of nominal Christians—will not be reaped until millions of laymen and lay women communicate the gospel effectively to responsive segments of the American population that lie all about them unreaped. Multiplication of congregations must become a part of the joyful obedience of every denomination, every seminary, every minister, and every Christian.

Too frequently the urgent need for such obedience is obscured by a hazy perspective of the picture. Too many Christians believe that far more people are practicing Christians than the facts indicate. I recently asked a man, "Are you a Christian?" "Yes," he replied, "of course I am. I'm an American, am I not?"

About thirty years ago I was doing some evangelistic calling in my neighborhood. I knocked on a door and was admitted and sat down for conversation with a genial businessman. After some preliminary conversation I invited him to come to my church.

"What denomination is it?" he asked.

"It is the Christian Church," I replied.

"Oh, thank you," he answered. "I wouldn't be interested. You see, I belong to the Methodist Church."

I switched the conversation immediately and a few moments later asked what Methodist church he belonged to. Please remember that this conversation was taking place in Oregon.

"Ah," he replied easily. "I am a member of the First Methodist Church in Miami, Florida."

Since I knew that he had come from Miami at least twenty years before, I knew that he was not a Methodist any more than I was a Hottentot! He was a lost soul.

Alas, it is too easy to assume that most people in America are Christians. Actually, the figures are quite different. As previously stated, perhaps only 50 million people in America are practicing Christians. A hundred million are nominal or marginal Christians. Many of them are highly secular and materialistic individuals who also belong to a church and attend worship now and then. About 90 million are not Christians at all. Many of them are convinced humanists or materialists. They never attend church and do not feel at all bound by biblical doctrine or morality. It is in this kind of a North America that Christians should plan their own obedience to the Great Commission. In a nation where at least 190 million need to be discipled, all schools of theological education must train ministers to become effective disciplers. Active and effective evangelism must become as real a part of the Christian life as honest conduct, telling the truth, sexual morality, the worship of God, and a correct understanding of *all* the Scriptures.

Effective evangelism, i.e., major church growth, is urgently needed in all cities of this great republic. Consequently, effective evangelism must become one of the main subjects taught in every school of theological education. The lost cannot be found unless every candidate for the ministry is taught how to find God's lost children and bring them home to their Father's house. He must also be taught how to multiply sound congregations in the multitudinous unchurched segments of American society.

4

Biblical Soundness, Spiritual Renewal, and Church Growth

Will biblical soundness and spiritual renewal *automatically* reap ripe harvest fields? It is at this precise point that many go astray. And so it is exactly here that we need careful thinking.

The Widespread Efforts Toward Doctrinal Soundness and Spiritual Renewal in North America and Other Lands

The last quarter of the twentieth century is seeing many movements toward renewal and many emphases on biblical soundness. These are occurring in all six continents among all branches of the universal church, both those which we consider biblically sound and those which we consider biblically questionable. The charismatic movement, which for many decades was limited to the Pentecostals, has now spread to denominations as separate as the Roman Catholic, Episcopalian, Methodist, Presbyterian, and Baptist.

Recently I received a request from the editor of a new denominational journal called *Disciple Renewal* to write an article for that paper. The editor and a group of ministers of the million-member Christian Church (Disciples of Christ) felt that the denomination as a whole needed a renewal movement in every state of the union. Their magazine was going to furnish one of the means for initiating, spreading, and supporting such a movement.

In the great United Methodist denomination a considerable number of congregations, feeling that the Board of Global Ministries was not sufficiently biblical and Spirit-filled, started a new missionary organization called The Mission Society for United Methodists. Presbyterians of both the former southern Presbyterian Church in the United States and northern Presbyterian Church in the United States of America have pulled out of those denominations and formed the Presbyterian Church in America, which claims to be a much sounder denomination. In the 1940s many withdrew from the Northern Baptist Church to form the Conservative Baptist denomination.

Often such movements aiming at biblical soundness and spiritual renewal occur within an existing denomination and intend to remain so. Often they split off to found new branches of the universal church, more orthodox or more Spirit-filled. Such movements are not limited to the United States. They go on in all countries of the world. Dr. David Barrett tells us that there are now 20,800 denominations in the world.[1] Many of these have arisen out of renewal movements that no longer felt comfortable in their old denominations. We must not let the fact that such multiplication of denominations seems questionable keep us from realizing that these movements are continually going on and are often animated by the best motives.

The Necessity of Biblical Soundness and Spiritual Renewal

Biblical soundness and spiritual renewal are highly necessary. Congregations and denominations do unfortunately, in some cases at least, grow cold. Under the impact of some new spurt of scholarship or of worldliness they become biblically unsound. They become so respectable, well organized, and academic that they attract only certain members of certain sections of the general population. Their congregations become sealed off and unreproductive. When the original members of such congregations move to the city or to the suburbs, the congregations do not attract the somewhat different kinds of people who have now moved into their places. Frequently whole denominations, despite some growing congregations, become static.

While I was speaking in some of the large cities of western Canada, I became aware that the strong Mennonite congregations in the

1. *World Christian Encyclopedia* (London: Oxford University Press, 1982), p. v.

farming communities were losing many of their younger members to the cities. These young, well-educated Mennonite men and women would move to the cities away from the farm, get urban jobs of one sort and another, and find themselves many miles from the nearest Mennonite congregation. Often maintaining stoutly that "We are Mennonites," they would continue to remain members of a far-off country church. And often they would lapse into nominal Christianity. Had the rural Mennonite congregation been fully biblical and spiritually renewed, they would have made every effort to multiply Mennonite congregations in the cities. They had many good starts, but they did not develop them. They not only would have shepherded scattered Mennonites but also would have won many of the secular nominally Christian and indeed pagan women and men living in the cities of North America and brought them to fervent belief in the Lord. The Mennonites were not biblically sound enough or spiritually filled enough to do this. Their experience is, alas, a common experience in too many denominations.

Renewal Often Concentrates on Existing Christians

Until the existing Christians become much more biblically sound and Spirit-filled than they now are, we must be concerned not with winning others but with reviving the saints. Believing this firmly in many places, renewal limits itself to existing Christians. This process is understandable. Existing congregations must become sounder, must know more of the Bible, must live more ardently Christian lives. Indeed, some Christians stridently maintain that until the church is purged of many of its nominal members, it can neither be the true church nor win others to true Christian faith. One of the notable criticisms of the church growth movement has been that what the church needs is not growth but a clearing out of many members who have no real faith in Christ.

We are speaking of the dual nature of biblical soundness and spiritual renewal. We certainly do and ought to motivate congregations and denominations to bring their present membership into a more ardent and doctrinally correct Christian life. This is what most sermons aim at. All Paul's letters are written to existing Christians and urge them to a deeper and more genuine Christian life. One aspect of biblical soundness and spiritual renewal certainly requires this.

However, we must look at the other side of biblical soundness and spiritual renewal. If anyone is really in Christ, if Christ does dwell in his heart through faith, he like Christ will seek the lost. He like Christ will look on fields white to harvest and work to bring in many sheaves. No one can be *fully* biblically sound and spiritually renewed without being tremendously concerned about the multitudes of unreached men and women and, indeed, of unreached segments of society. It is impossible for anybody to be really in Christ, really full of the Holy Spirit, without doing what the 120 did on the day of Pentecost. They rushed out and told everyone they met about Jesus and urged them to become His followers. They spoke to Jews from fifteen different countries living in Jerusalem, in addition to those born in Palestine. Three thousand were added to the church in one day.

When anyone gives his life entirely to Christ, he does what Paul did. He devotes himself to multiplying churches in other segments of the population. He notes the segments of society in his neighborhood that are unchurched. He looks at the 75-80 percent of the American population that are not in Christ. He notes that they are in many cases highly winnable. He lifts up his eyes and looks on the fields and sees that many of them are white to harvest. He hurries off to get his sickle and rope in order to bind up sheaves and carry them back to the Master's barn. He notes that 4 billion today and 5 billion tomorrow of the world's population are not Christians in any sense, and he resolves to do his part to bring them to salvation.

Men and women who are biblically sound and spiritually renewed will certainly live genuinely Christian lives. They will also demonstrate that the genuine Christian life is always concerned with and works at bringing God's lost children back to their Father's house. The dual nature of biblical soundness and spiritual renewal guarantees that vital Christians will not focus on themselves and nominal Christians only. They seek to be biblically sound in regard to bringing in the sheaves and spiritually renewed in regard to multiplying churches.

Only a Growing Congregation Is Fully Sound and Fully Renewed

Biblical soundness and spiritual renewal require activity on both fronts—Christians must become more moral and devout, *and they must become more effective harvesters.* Here again we must see what happened on the day of Pentecost. The 120 had been meeting in secret. They had been afraid that, like their Master, they would be persecuted and indeed killed by the Jews. But when the Holy Spirit came upon them, they went public in a very big way. They rushed out into the streets. They started telling people that Jesus Christ was not dead. God had raised Him from the dead, and all ought to become His followers. The account in Acts 2 is certainly clear that all of the 120 started speaking to everybody on the streets of Jerusalem. Normally retiring men spoke boldly to anyone they met. Modest and even timid women started to tell those they met about Jesus. They were imparting great good news. They were telling others of the way of salvation. They were sharing the most important news they had ever received. All of them—women and men, leaders and followers, extroverts and introverts—they all stopped anyone they met and said excitedly to him or her, "Let me tell you of the most important thing that has happened in many years. Have you heard the amazing good news? This is something you absolutely must hear. I know you're busy, but you will never forgive yourself if you do not stop and listen."

Indeed, so unusual was this excited communication that many of those to whom they spoke exclaimed, "We must not take all this excitement too seriously. These people have simply drunk too much. They are talking nonsense."

When a vast crowd, perhaps ten thousand men and women, had gathered, Peter then spoke to them the message recorded in Acts 2. Many of the crowd were deeply touched and exclaimed, "What must we then do?"

Peter replied, Believe on the Lord Jesus Christ. Be baptized and become His confessed followers.

It is not necessary to believe that 100 percent biblical soundness and spiritual renewal issue in an exact duplication of these events. These events were suited to the situation in ancient Jerusalem seven weeks after the crucifixion of the Lord Jesus. But biblical soundness and spiritual renewal will result in speaking to modern men and women around us in ways suited to their situations. Full biblical soundness and spiritual renewal will never permit Christians to make no effort whatever to communicate the faith and say comfortably, "That is the business of the pastor and Billy Graham."

Let me give you an example of what happened in far-off India in 1933. In the town of Yeotmal a small Free Methodist congregation had been formed. It was being addressed by a notable preacher. His words carried great conviction. The members were filled with the Holy Spirit. In addition to forgiving each other and manifesting an utterly new warmth and reality of Christian life, they felt that they must communicate the gospel to other people. So the whole congregation, men and women, every evening at five o'clock would assemble just outside the county courthouse. As the hundreds who worked there were leaving for home, they saw people singing Christ's praises and telling about the Lord Jesus and the way of salvation.

The clerks, lawyers, and government officials working in the courthouse had never heard anything like this before. They clustered around each group of Christians, listening to what they had to say. They all agreed that these Christians had had a very remarkable experience. They were impressed by what they heard. After fifteen or twenty minutes the Christians said, "We will be back tomorrow to tell you more." These meetings every evening continued for over a month. But none of the listeners confessed Christ and became Christians. At that time in that part of India such a step was to them unthinkable.

Gradually the crowds grew smaller and smaller. The Christians came to feel that they had done their part, and the proclamation on the courthouse steps ceased. Pentecost had come and gone without any conversions. The renewed Christians had spoken to an unresponsive audience.

Then one of the Christians, perhaps more deeply moved than the others, resolved to go from village to village in the country district surrounding the town. Every night as the villagers gathered before they went to bed, he would tell them of the Lord Jesus. They listened with great interest, but there were no conversions for more than a month. Then he came to a village near which coal had been discovered and a mining operation was in progress. The miners were members of a caste which, two hundred miles to the south, had become largely Christian. When they heard, they said, "Many of our own people have become Christian. Becoming Christians has been very good for them. They have built churches and are living renewed lives. This is truly good news. We too will become followers of the Lord Jesus." Several new congregations were established.

In short, those who would proclaim Jesus Christ must not only proclaim but must proclaim intelligently. They must distinguish between fields ripe to harvest and fields that are yet unplowed. World evangelization or the effective discipling of unreached segments of society must be an intelligent operation, not a blind one. We are to pray the Lord of the harvest to send laborers into ripe fields.

The world is full of ripe fields. It is also full of many unripe fields and many that have not even been plowed. Biblically sound and revived Christians must act intelligently. They must seek God's guidance and go to the ripe fields. It is only out of ripe fields that they can bring in one sheaf a minute.

We must not limit renewal and revival to care of existing Christians. This truth bears restatement. It is so easy for revival to concern itself chiefly with the people who are already in the church building. They form the close community in which everybody knows everybody else. It is among members of this community that love, justice, brotherhood, and forgiveness are most easily exercised. To be sure, revival must begin with existing Christians. Renewal started in the 120 gathered in the upper room, but the revival did not end there. The revived must reach out to multitudes of other people. They must multiply worshiping congregations in their own and other segments of society.

We remember Paul's strategy, "I have become all things to all men so that by all possible means I might save some" (1 Cor. 9:22) and his exhortation, "Follow my example" (1 Cor. 11:1). He was answering the questions as to whether Christians should eat meat offered to idols. The only place where Christians would be offered that kind of food would be in the homes of non-Christians. The Christians would be meeting other kinds of people. Paul says that, when Christians are served meat at the table, they should not ask if it has been offered to idols. They should just eat it. They do not know that it has been offered to idols. If, however, someone says that it has been offered to idols, then "do not eat it, both for the sake of the man who told you and for conscience' sake—the other man's conscience, I mean, not yours. . . . even as I try to please everybody in every way. . . . so that they may be saved. Follow my example" (1 Cor. 10:28ff.).

That command needs to be obeyed by all faculties and student bodies in seminaries. All ministerial candidates need to be carefully instructed in the many ways in which they can reach out and be all things to all men in order to win some. Only when pastors and ministers in all denominations are effectively multiplying congregations in unreached segments of the population will eternal God's command be carried out. Only then will Christians become much more effective evangelists.

A *full* infilling of the Holy Spirit and *full* biblical obedience will always be deeply concerned that the unsaved hear and obey the gospel.

If we are to be biblically sound, we must reach out to the unsaved. We must discern ripe harvest fields. We must motivate ourselves, our students, and the members of our churches to recognize the unsaved and to tell them of the way to salvation. We must recognize that the greatest danger facing practicing Christians is to practice their Christianity among themselves, to tell the good news only to those who come to their church, and to be unconcerned about those who do not.

This danger faces Bible colleges and seminaries also. They believe that future pastors must have precise knowledge of correct doctrines and must themselves be spiritually renewed. Otherwise they cannot adequately care for their congregations. This is certainly true. However, it totally omits the equally important fact that they must search for, find, and bring back to His house multitudes of the Father's lost children. Theological seminaries cannot—repeat, cannot—be theologically correct unless they realize that theological correctness and spiritual vitality require a constant concern for the unsaved. Pastors and ministers in training must learn how congregations that have never planted a daughter church, that have been barren, can multiply churches among the 4 billion unsaved, which now form four-fifths of the world's population. Leaders of the church must know how to wake sleeping churches and to make them evangelistically much more effective.

Some years ago when I was speaking at a church growth seminar held in an Ohio town, one of the influential ministers in the town said to me, "I shall attend the seminar, but I am not really convinced that it is needed. Surely we have plenty of churches in this town, and every church is very cordial to all those who come. Most churches will see that visitors are called upon by either the minister or members of the evangelistic committee. We do not need to increase the number of congregations in this town. There are too many already."

In preparation for the opening session I spent the next two days assembling some data—the population of the town, the number of churches, the seating capacity of each. At the first session of the seminar, without referring to this minister at all, I said, "In this town you have thirty thousand residents. There are sixty-one churches. Less than six thousand men and women are to be found in these churches on Sunday; twenty-four thousand will not be in church. Granted that church members number somewhat more than six thousand, it nevertheless seems perfectly clear that at least half and possibly two-thirds of the people in this town have yet to become genuine followers of Christ. This is the reason why you should emphasize church growth."

Revival and doctrinal soundness must not be limited to the six thousand who will be in church on Sunday. It must begin there, to be sure, but it must reach out to the twenty-four thousand. They are God's children.

Conversion Growth Essential

Another reason why biblical soundness and spiritual renewal many times do not bring church growth is that seminaries, ministers, and lay leaders seldom realize that no amount of biological growth and transfer growth will carry out the Great Commission.

All growth of the church may be divided into three categories—biological, transfer, and conversion. By *biological church growth* we mean that children of existing Christians come to have Christian faith because they are born into Christian families, go to church as children, come to believe on Christ as children, are later confirmed or baptized, and become confessing members of living congregations. They yield themselves to Christ and come to know a great deal of the Bible. But this is a gradual process. Since such growth plays no part in winning the 4 billion outside the church to Christ, we place it in a special category—biological growth. To be sure, no following of Christ can be strictly a biological process. Some children of Christian parents reject Christ. All those who become Christians must themselves take a final conclusive step of faith and obedience. Nevertheless, the phrase "biological church growth" is valuable since it enables us to classify one kind of Christian.

In the second kind of growth, *transfer growth*, Christians from New York move to Fort Worth. They leave their New York congregations and join Fort Worth congregations. The Fort Worth congregations record additions of perhaps twenty and perhaps one hundred members during a given year. However, transfer growth, while it adds to individual congregations, adds nothing at all to total membership of the denomination concerned. Indeed, since many Christians are lost in transit, transfer causes considerable loss.

The third kind of church growth, *conversion growth*, results from winning the lost. These may be nominal or lapsed Christians, secularists, agnostics, or atheists. They may also be Muslims, Hindus, Jews, or other non-Christians. When doctrinal soundness and spiritual renewal win the lost, multiply new congregations in unchurched populations, and effectively evangelize the unreached, then they carry out God's continuing purpose to find *and fold* lost sheep.

Too often ministers and lay leaders and professors in theological schools, as well, limit their expectations to growth from biological and transfer sources. These are important. Nevertheless, until substantial conversion growth as defined above occurs, the astronomical numbers of the unreached remain very largely unreached.

In short, doctrinal soundness and spiritual renewal must always aim at substantial numbers of conversions from the unreached. Any congregation, denomination, or theological seminary that would be true to the biblical imperatives must insist that full doctrinal soundness by itself impels Christians to seek the lost, to evangelize the unreached, to multiply congregations among the unchurched, and to engage continually in planned, prayer-supported, and effective world evangelization. All those concerned with spiritual renewal should make doubly sure that spiritual renewal does not limit itself to revivifying of the already saved. Spiritual renewal must send waves of the renewed out to search for the lost. Otherwise, it is only partial renewal.

Any theological school aiming to prepare pastors, preachers, or ministers must include several four-hour courses on effective evangelism. The enormous number of ministers who obtain little conversion growth must be reduced. Graduates of seminaries must go out well equipped to multiply new congregations among unreached, non-Christian segments of the population. As I write these sentences I have before me a letter from a pastor in Hawaii saying that he has just taken up new duties in a church that has been there for one hundred years and has never planted a daughter church. Many graduates of many seminaries go to just such congregations. If they are to turn their congregations around, if those churches are to cease being barren and to become fruitful, Bible colleges and seminaries must make effective evangelism one of their main emphases.

5

How Can We Assure Effective Evangelism?

How can we make sure that the ripe fields in every state of the union—and indeed every country of the world—are reaped? I lay before you seven urgent steps. Be assured that many more than seven could be mentioned, but these are vitally important.

1. Emphasize the Tremendous Evangelistic Passion of the New Testament Church

The New Testament church spread amazingly. It multiplied itself beyond belief. Not only did it run through the Jewish population, but it spread to the Samaritan people and to the officers of the occupying Roman Army. When the official leaders, apostles, deacons, and elders of the existing Jewish churches were working busily in Jerusalem and Judea, some very ordinary Christians, "men of Cyprus and Cyrene went to Antioch and began to speak to Greeks also" (Acts 11:20). The gospel was also carried to Rome by unnamed lay Christians long before Paul arrived there. In short, New Testament Christians, laymen as well as apostles, were tremendously concerned that people outside the church—non-Christians, secularists, materialists, followers of other religions—hear about the only true religion, come to know the only Savior, believe upon Him, and be baptized in His name.

In our preaching let us make sure that this aspect of the Christian faith is repeatedly held up before our congregations, Sunday school meetings, and other assemblies of the saints. To be a true church we must become a reproductive church. Let us remember that full biblical soundness and spiritual renewal *cannot* limit themselves to existing congregations. They must multiply congregations. They

45

must win non-Christian men and women in many locations. This teaching must become an essential part of all theological instruction.

2. In Every Congregation Form a Missionary Group Intent on Multiplying Churches Among the Unreached in Its Own and Other Nations

In any congregation there will be some who are ardent believers and others whose faith is less glowing. Let the ardent Christians form missionary groups or evangelistic bands that will meet once a week or once a month to make sure that "our congregation does win the lost in our community and give birth to daughter congregations at home and abroad." Every living congregation should have a band of members who meet regularly to plan and carry out systematic propagation of the gospel. They will make sure that not only do they believe in Christ in regard to these matters, but they obey Him. They will see that the teaching of the Bible glows with evangelistic passion.

This is particularly necessary because, alas, it is possible to teach great sections of the Bible without ever mentioning eternal God's command to make the gospel known to all segments of society. Ardent local missionary groups will make sure that that does not happen in their congregations. Unless such bands are formed, there is a danger that all the teachings and activities of the church are concentrated upon the existing members of the church and those visitors who return to it. Evangelistic bands and missionary-minded men and women will help assure that this does not happen.

3. Send Out Sons and Daughters of the Congregation as Missionaries to Disciple Particular Ethne

I have been greatly grieved at the large numbers of congregations in North America from which in the past thirty years no son or daughter of the church has become a lifetime evangelist or missionary. Unfortunately, a very large percentage of American congregations would fall into this class. But they do not need to. As Bible colleges and seminaries begin recognizing the deplorable situation and training prospective ministers, congregations and whole denominations will begin to surge forward.

Suppose an essential element of being Christian was held to be leading a member of one's own congregation to be a missionary. What a revolution would take place! Suppose that every hundred practicing Episcopalians or Presbyterians or Lutherans would send out from among themselves one missionary, either to the unchurched in their own neighborhood or nation or to the unchurched in some other nation. What an enormous expansion of the church would soon ensue! Is this an impossibility? Is it financially unthinkable? By no means. A hundred Christians could without much financial stress send out, fund, and maintain one lifetime worker. Doing that would not in the least exhaust their tithe, and such a move would make sure that the church of Jesus Christ would at long last take seriously the ripe fields stretching away on all sides to the horizons.

4. Become Well Acquainted With the Ethne Being Discipled

Kittel defines an *ethnos* as a group of like individuals. A swarm of bees is spoken of as an *ethnos*. So is a herd of cattle. An *ethnos* of men is a segment of society. The Greek word *ethnos* has been correctly translated in India's fifteen major languages as *jati* or caste. Tribes, castes, classes, segments of society—these are the *ethne* of which the population of the world consists. Every congregation should focus its attention on one or more *ethne* at home or abroad.

Some years ago several denominations in Canada began to see the French Canadians as an unreached *ethnos* and to plan to evangelize French Canadians (most of whom are very nominal Catholics), encouraging them to form French-speaking, Bible-believing congregations. These would be led by French-speaking pastors, elders, and deacons. In such congregations members speaking politically could advocate that French-speaking Canada form a separate nation. They could advocate this and still remain quite respectable, well-loved members of the church. Were French Canadians to become members of Anglo churches, they could not advocate any such political position without exciting severe antagonism on the part of their fellow Christians.

The French Canadians are an *ethnos* that must be reached in ways
that fit that *ethnos*. There are similar *ethne* in all the cities of the
United States and indeed in the world. In all of them there are many
communities in which large numbers of the residents are not practicing Christians. Many among these can be won today and tomorrow.

5. Give Substantially to That Work and Pray Continuously for It

Any serious effort to reap ripe fields will require financial under-
girding. When we pray the Lord of the harvest to send laborers into
the harvest, we are also praying that He will motivate existing
Christians, congregations, and conferences to give sacrificially to
that end. I am speaking to Americans, the most financially secure of
any citizenry in the world. Our Christian faith will be tested by the
degree to which we undergird effective evangelism at home and
abroad. Let us make sure that at this point our plans are both
biblically correct and financially responsible.

6. Assemble Accurate Information as to the Degree and Kind of Discipling Actually Being Achieved and Constantly Convey This Information to the Congregation and Denomination

This aspect of the Christian enterprise is one that is frequently
overlooked. We must reap ripe harvest fields; *but we must not work
blindfolded*. We must find out which are the ripest fields, the most
readily reached, the paths to and from the barn that are most suited
to those carrying heavy sheaves. We must not send the largest
number of laborers into unripe fields to water or weed them. We
must measure accurately what needs to be done. We must make
sure that sickles are kept sharp. We must have a record as to the
number of sheaves each worker brings in, and we must not stack oat
sheaves and wheat sheaves indiscriminately together. Farmers store
oats, wheat, barley, and corn in separate parts of the barn.

The figures of speech just used will illustrate the tasks that must
be done. The world is full of receptive and resistant populations.
While all must hear the gospel (Mark 16:14), we must make sure that

the ripe fields are the ones that are reaped to the last sheaf. It is at this point that schools of theological education need to be particularly alert. Among the hundreds of segments of the American people, which ones are most responsive to the gospel? Among which can congregations be multiplied most certainly? What are the most effective methods of multiplying? What methods guarantee that no multiplication of congregations will take place? Where is great reaping going on? And where are the unsown fields from which reapers must turn and to which plowmen must be sent?

Paul wanted to go into Bithynia, but the Lord would not permit it. Where are our Bithynias from which the Lord Himself turns us?

In all these and kindred matters we need light upon what is actually happening, upon where the church is growing, where congregations are multiplying, and where they are not. We need accurate information on what kind of seminary graduates multiply congregations, and what kind of seminary graduates do not multiply congregations; what kind of teaching produces men able to win others, and what kind of teaching produces men who will talk learnedly on sacred subjects but will inspire no one to win others.

Accurate portrayal of all these essential points enables intelligent action. Instead of working blindfolded, we must know the exact situation. When God's people see the truth in regard to these matters, they can and will act intelligently and responsibly. This is the basic reason why research into these essential matters is so urgently required by Bible schools, theological seminaries, missionary societies, synods, presbyteries, and congregations.

7. Create and Set to Work Large, Effective Lay Evangelistic Forces

In too many congregations, denominations, and schools of theological education evangelism is thought to be the work of a few ardent ministers to whom God has given the gift of evangelism and who become professional evangelists. Evangelism is thought to be the exclusive work of men such as John Wesley, Billy Sunday, Billy Graham, and many others. In most congregations there are few members, if any, working at winning the lost and incorporating them into Christ's body, the church. It is commonly believed that those congregations grow whose ministers preach appealing, interesting, humorous, and powerful sermons. If you want the church to grow, build an attractive building, make sure that visitors are welcomed, let the pastor call on all newcomers to the community, and have a superior choir. All these are good activities, but if any congregation limits itself to these, very few of its members, if any, will devote themselves to effective evangelism.

In sharp distinction to the foregoing is that pattern wherein large numbers of devoted Christian women and men systematically work at communicating the gospel to their unbelieving neighbors, friends, and fellow citizens. In order to do this they must, of course, be trained. Most ordinary Christians, no matter how earnestly Christian they are, find it embarrassing to talk to neighbors about accepting Jesus Christ as Lord and Savior. They can talk about the weather, politics, baseball, or football, or the latest crimes. But about becoming believing, practicing Christians they talk with difficulty, if at all.

This tremendous lack is remarkable in view of the biblical record of the New Testament church. On the day of Pentecost all the 120—women as well as men, ordinary Christians as well as apostles—surged out to the streets to tell people that the Lord had risen. It was unnamed laymen who, on coming to Antioch, initiated a brand new kind of church growth. They spoke not only to the Jews but also to the Greeks. Those who planted perhaps six or more house churches in Rome before Paul arrived there were not apostles; they were ordinary Christians.

Every great expansion of the church in all ages has depended upon the Word being spread by believing Christians of all ranks. Conversely, whenever effective evangelism has been held to be the work solely of trained evangelists and paid pastors, there denominations have grown slowly or have become static or declined.

Consequently, every school that prepares pastors and ministers should teach all students how to train laywomen and laymen to be effective evangelists. This will not be done by professors or pastors who have never won anybody to Christ.

Every seminary should teach every ministerial candidate how to speak courteously and persuasively to several different segments of society. When these candidates become ministers themselves, they will be able to teach their members. Nongrowing congregations will rapidly become growing congregations.

Some may, however, object, saying, "Scripture tells us that the gift of evangelism is given only to some people." This is quite true. Those to whom the gift of evangelism is given will become much more effective evangelists than others. We rejoice in this fact. However, it does not in the least contradict the biblical imperative that every Christian is commanded to be a witness. Furthermore, we need not suppose that nothing will happen until *all* the members of a congregation go out and speak to unbelievers about Christ. Quite on the contrary, if only one out of ten in any congregation becomes effectively evangelistic, that congregation will grow. The church of Jesus Christ will certainly treasure great evangelists like John Knox, Billy Graham, and others. But it will also train at least 10 percent of its members to speak courteously and persuasively to the lost in their neighborhoods. The church will not assume that men who have never handled a sickle can be effective reapers. It will train people to use sickles effectively.

Referring to the previous chapter on biblical soundness and spiritual renewal, let me ask, Will these automatically bring church growth? The answer is both no and yes. If we mean biblical soundness with respect to doctrines that have little bearing on evangelization, the answer is no. If spiritual renewal is limited to those inside church buildings, then the answer is no. But if biblical soundness continually emphasizes the overwhelming concern of God that His Son be made known to all humanity and that His plan of salvation be presented to all everywhere and that *panta ta ethne* be incorporated into Christ's body, then the answer is certainly yes. If spiritual renewal means that renewed Christians surge out in the most enlightened way possible, guided by the most exact information available, to share the way of life with all men and women everywhere, then the answer is certainly yes. Let us make sure that all biblical soundness is fully biblical and our spiritual renewal does send us out to the fields ripe to harvest. Let us not be embarrassed in rescuing the perishing and caring for the dying.

Conclusion

By implementing the seven measures we have discussed, every congregation and every denomination, every minister, and every school of theological education can help bring about effective evangelism. Such evangelism must not simply be talked about in special lectures and in evangelism classes. It must be carried out in the field. It will cost blood, sweat, toil, and tears. But it will also evoke the blessed words, "Well done, good and faithful servant," from the Lord of the harvest.

6

The Rise of the Church Growth Movement

The preceding chapters have insisted that the discipling of all the peoples of earth is commanded by God and will not be brought about by what commonly passes for full doctrinal correctness and spiritual renewal. We have faced frankly the fact that much sound but partial Christianity today does not result in winning many of the lost or bringing many sheaves of ripe grain into the Lord's barn. This chapter tells of my personal pilgrimage as I faced these facts and tried to devise appropriate actions. Some similar pilgrimage will be the experience of all those who turn from nongrowing conventional or ardent Christianity to carrying out the command of the ultimate Authority in the universe. The church growth movement is addressed to the fact that the most powerful world church ever to exist is, in many cases, either slow growing or declining. It is hoped that this personal view of the rise of the church growth movement will help focus attention on the amazingly receptive world and the urgency of reaping ripe fields and the absolute necessity of making theological curricula suited to today's opportunities.

My pilgrimage in the twentieth century resulted from eternal God's command. In Romans 16:25,26 God commands that the gospel be made known to all peoples (segments of society), leading them to faith and obedience. Every segment of society—rural and urban, literate and illiterate, high income and low income, factory workers and university professors—must hear the gospel. It must be proclaimed with the purpose of discipling every piece of the human mosaic, with the intention to make it a Christian segment of humanity. This command must be seen against the enormous number of God's lost children. Four-fifths of all humankind do not yet believe in Jesus Christ; they have not yet been saved. Christians must, of course, be concerned to lead thoroughly Christian lives. They must also realize that any such life must devote a large part of its thoughts, labors, and prayers to winning men and women to Christ and multiplying churches.

The Theological River of Thought

My pilgrimage was greatly influenced by three rivers of thought that dominated the twentieth century. The first was a theological river. At the beginning of the century most Christians and most ministers were distinctly biblical in their emphasis. As decade succeeded decade, however, historical and literary criticism of the Bible produced in many denominations a sharp diminution of the authority of Scripture. Since literary critics held that the Bible was made up of many different strands written by different authors at different times (J, E, D, P, Q, and the rest), it was increasingly easy for some Christians to emphasize those sections of Scripture that appealed to them and write off the rest as not authentic and infallible revelation.

For example, a professor in a neighboring theological seminary to whom I had quoted John 14:6 replied, "Well, McGavran, that verse does say that no one comes to the Father 'but by me,' but we must all recognize that at that point the latest editor of the book of John was waxing somewhat enthusiastic." Against this liberal current, Westminster, Trinity, and many other evangelical schools of theological education were founded.

My pilgrimage was tremendously influenced both by eternal God's command and by the currents of theological opinion for and against biblical authority, which have ebbed and flowed throughout the twentieth century.

The missionary movement in 1900 was carried on chiefly by the great missionary societies of the older Protestant churches. As a result of the end of the imperial era and increasing liberalization and other forces these societies gradually diminished their missionary labors. Conservative evangelical missionary societies gradually *increased* theirs. My Christian faith and ministry have developed through the years in the midst of these great tides of conviction.

In the summer of 1919, shortly after I had been discharged from the army, on my return from France I decided that God was calling me to full-time Christian service. In December of that year at the Student Volunteer Convention in Des Moines, Iowa, I decided to become a lifetime missionary. I was then president of the senior class at Butler College in Indianapolis, Indiana. Immediately on graduating in the summer of 1920 I entered Yale Divinity School and graduated *cum laude* in 1922. While there my professors, all of whom had studied in Germany and were theological liberals and "modern scholars," had convinced me of the truth of the liberal position. The Bible that I read for the next fifteen years had the various strands (J, E, D, P, etc.) underlined in different colors.

Nevertheless, since my work during those years lay in India and was carried on in the Hindi language, and since I was quite sure that the idol worshipers whom I addressed needed to abandon their idols to worship the true God revealed in the Bible and in Jesus Christ, the liberal position did not greatly affect my thoughts. I used the Bible, read from it, and quoted it precisely as any evangelical Christian would. But in the back of my mind theological liberalism persisted as my understanding of the truth.

This liberal position was reemphasized in 1930 when Mrs. Mc-Gavran and I returned to America on our first furlough. I had been awarded a research fellowship at Union Theological Seminary in New York, an ardently liberal institution. While I was studying there for my Ph.D., almost everything I heard and read reflected the liberal position.

On our return to India in October 1932 I was elected field secretary of the seventy-missionary India Mission of the United Christian Missionary Society of Indianapolis. This required much travel to all of our various stations. It also required that, when I was in Jubbulpore, our headquarters, I teach a Sunday school class of the men of the church. These were mostly men with an average education of seventh or eighth grade. My predecessor, Dr. William McDougall, had been a flaming liberal, a graduate of Chicago Divinity School. He had taught this Bible class for the previous seven years.

A turning point in my theological pilgrimage took place one Sunday morning when I asked the class of some fifteen or twenty men, "When you read a biblical passage such as we are studying this morning, what is the first question you ask?"

One of the most intelligent replied immediately, "What is there in this passage that we cannot believe?" What he meant, of course, was that when we read the passage about Jesus walking on the water, we know instantly that He could not have done that. Consequently, we must understand the passage as an exaggerated or poetic representation of what happened.

I had never before been confronted so bluntly with what the liberal position means to ordinary Christians in multitudinous instances. It shocked me, and I began at that moment to sense that it could not be the truth. Despite all the difficulties, I began to feel my way back toward convictions concerning the Bible as infallible revelation. It is God's Word. It is entirely dependable. It is the rule of faith and practice of every true Christian.

Since my work after 1935 lay chiefly with illiterate idol-worshiping peasants in the great plain of Chhattisgarh, this conviction expressed itself not in sermons, dissertations, or articles written for professors in theological schools but rather in messages to the segment of society to whose evangelization God had sent me.

For example, I found that when I told the story of the cross to most village audiences, whether of non-Christians or Christians, they were likely to respond: "Well, they caught up with the poor man and killed him. That is exactly what the Hindus did to some of our own religious leaders." Consequently, when I prepared the outlines of twelve Bible accounts that were to be learned (indeed, memorized) by village congregations and came to the outline of the story of the cross, I wrote the following four sentences, which the village pastor was to use word for word and which his congregations were to memorize word for word. If they did this, they would think of the crucifixion in its true sense. They could never again say, "They caught up with the poor fellow and killed him." The four sentences read as follows:

> The Lord Jesus Christ was God incarnate. With one word he could have burned up all those who were crucifying Him—the Sanhedrin, Pilate, the Roman soldiers, and all the rest. But He came not to destroy people but to save them. So He died in our place there on the cross.

I rejected the moral theory of the atonement, which had been taught at Yale Divinity School. I accepted the substitutionary view of the atonement, which the Bible so clearly expresses.

My renewed conviction concerning biblical authority also motivated my concepts concerning missionary labors of all kinds. I saw clearly that unless the Bible was accepted as God's authoritative, infallible revelation, there was no reason at all for missionary labors. Instead, let the people of each great religion move forward at their own pace, reforming their own religion, and gradually growing into a unified world society. I came to see that any real missionary movement must depend upon an authoritative Word of God made known in the Bible and manifested by our Lord and Savior Jesus Christ.

This is the only theological position that makes the communication of the gospel, the discipling of *panta ta ethne*, the multiplication of congregations in every segment of all societies, essential. This is the theological conviction underlying the church growth movement.

To the extent that this theological conviction is weakened, effective evangelism necessarily declines. Why should anybody seek to win his unbelieving neighbors or go to a foreign land and learn a foreign language unless it is indeed true that He to whom all authority in heaven and earth is given has commanded us to *matheteusate panta ta ethne* (disciple all the peoples)?

The Second River of Thought

The second river of thought in which all evangelistic labor in the twentieth century has been carried on consists of *knowing* the religious beliefs, cultural customs, physical resources, and ways of living of the segment of society being evangelized. In the first half of the century it was considered essential for the evangelist to know the religion of the population he or she evangelized. Were the person going to China, he or she had to become well versed in Confucian and Buddhist thought. In Africa, Islam or animism had to be known; in India, Hinduism or Islam; and in Latin America, Roman Catholicism.

After 1950 or thereabouts, however, because of the tremendous popularity of anthropology in state universities, the need to know other religions was largely supplanted by the need to know anthropology, i.e., the culture of the people being evangelized. Since most of the tremendous advances of the Christian faith in the twentieth century had taken place among animist tribal populations, which had few, if any, religious books or well-stated theological systems, anthropology did indeed furnish greater understanding of the peoples concerned.

The first professor whom I called to the faculty of the School of World Mission was Dr. Alan Tippett, Ph.D. in anthropology and for twenty years an ardent missionary in the Fiji Islands. If one is going to disciple any animistic tribe, he should certainly know its way of thinking, living, and acting—in short, its culture. The same is certainly true of any pastor ministering within the various cultures in any of our fifty states.

To evangelize Muslims, Hindus, Buddhists, Communists, or adherents of any other religion, one must know their religious beliefs. He must have read their books and know their values and systems of theology and philosophy.

In the first half of the twentieth century, part of the preparation of my colleagues in the India Mission of the United Christian Missionary Society of Indianapolis was to read a Hindi book called *Shad Darshan Darpan*, which described the six most common systems of Hindu philosophy. My own doctoral dissertation (1932) described nineteen major beliefs of Hinduism and the effect Christian education had on high school boys holding these beliefs.

When in 1966 the accrediting committee of the Western Association of Schools and Colleges visited the Fuller School of World Mission, it was displeased that it did not find us teaching comparative religions. "How," exclaimed one of its members, "can you run a school of missions and not teach comparative religions?"

As the church growth movement took shape in my mind between 1933 and 1953, it was greatly influenced by this second river. An effective discipler of *panta ta ethne* must know the religions, cultures, occupations, and ways of living of those to whom he preaches Christ. He will be forming congregations of a specific kind of people. Those in Florida will be somewhat different from those in North Dakota. That is why the church growth school of thought constantly emphasizes that each segment of society as it becomes Christian will look somewhat different from other segments of society that become Christian. The church—the body of Christ—is indeed one; but like the human body it has many different parts. Denominations made up very largely of illiterate landless laborers in Malaysia are not likely to look or sound like denominations made up of college graduates in upper-middle-class American society. Fingernails do not look or feel like eyes, but they are both integral parts of the body. The church growth movement urges that people become sincere practicing Christians while remaining ethnically, culturally, and economically themselves. In India this meant that vegetarian societies should remain vegetarian. There is no need for a cultural component to be changed to fit the meat-eating habits of European populations.

As Christianity is thereby encouraged to flow into many different populations at home and abroad and men and women are enabled to become Christian while remaining culturally themselves, the church growth movement believes that many more will become disciples of the Lord Jesus. For example, it is not necessary for Africans who become Christians to become Westerners, moderns, or highly educated, as long as they put aside all other gods, all other scriptures, believe on Jesus Christ as God and Savior, and accept the Bible as their rule of faith and practice. They can become good Christians no matter what their culture, tongue, education, or political power happens to be.

This is particularly important in urban evangelization in the United States. Despite the fact that in America we are all one people, the urban populations are composed of many different segments. The ethnic minorities living in inner cities are quite different from the wealthy populations in beautiful suburbs. What well-paid, well-educated, comfortably housed American Christians can afford by way of church buildings ought not to determine the places of assembly of Christian congregations living on the edge of poverty in inner-city ghettos. We all must remember that New Testament churches never built a single church building. Many congregations in American cities cannot afford to erect buildings. Thoroughly Christian congregations that meet in rented quarters, in homes, and the like must be regarded as one form of the church fitting certain economically disadvantaged segments of the population. In short, the physical form of the congregation will vary enormously as the multitudinous segments of the world's populations—the multitudinous *ethne*—are discipled.

The Third River of Thought

A third river of thought also greatly influenced my pilgrimage. This river consisted of an accurate account of the growth rate and patterns of the new churches being multiplied. Responsible stewards of God's grace must assemble an accurate picture of those turning to Christ and passing from death to life. They must know whether the church is growing at 2 percent or 200 percent a decade.

As theological convictions formed in my mind and grew clearer and more definite year by year, I saw that in a great majority of cases missionaries in Asia, Africa, and Latin America, the lands I knew and in which I traveled, were indeed doing many good works—education, medicine, literacy, uplift, rural reconstruction, and the like—but in too many instances they were not being very effective in winning people to Christ, e.g., they were not obeying Christ's command. They were not acutely conscious of the number of sheaves they were bringing to the Master's barn. Gradually I came to believe that every missionary and minister, every congregation, and indeed every sincere Christian must be tremendously concerned that the gospel be made known to and believed by many of his non-Christian, secular, agnostic, or atheistic neighbors and friends.

In 1934 I discovered that in mid-India, where I then lived, many missionary societies from the United States, Sweden, England, Canada, and the like were at work in 145 towns and cities. In only eleven of these was the Christian population growing satisfactorily. *In 134 cases the Christian population was increasing at less than 1 percent a year!*

In 1934 also the mid India Christian Council invited J. Waskom Pickett, a Methodist missionary who had just published his book, *Christian Mass Movements in India,* to do a survey of seven mission stations of seven different missions—one each from the United Church of Canada, the Mennonite, the Evangelical Synod, the

Christian Church, and the Anglican Church, and two from the Methodist Episcopal Church. The council asked me to accompany him. I observed carefully what he found out in four of these areas. He then asked me to complete the survey using his methods.

All of this cast a great deal of light upon why the church was growing in only a few stations. As I studied missions in other lands, I found the same thing was true. Most of this slow growth was explained on the basis that existing religions were tremendously opposed to any spread of Christianity. This was true in some cases. However, in many others the lack of growth was due to preventable causes. In some cases less than 10 percent of the total resources of the missions and denominations was spent on effective evangelism. In other cases where a church had grown strong in one segment of society, "becoming a Christian" to other segments of society meant "leaving our people to join that other segment." Scores of other reasons practically guaranteed that sincere, devoted mission work led to very little church growth.

The church growth movement, in consequence, has greatly emphasized accurate research into the effectiveness of church and mission labors. It insists not only that the amount and rate of growth must be accurately charted, but also that the real reasons for growth or lack of growth must be accurately known. In almost every nation some evangelism is attended by rapid church growth; but much evangelism is attended by very little. Christians must describe and memorize the causes of both growth and nongrowth. Those intending to obey eternal God's command to disciple all the peoples of earth must know which of the peoples are ready for discipling and which are resolutely opposed to it, which fields are white to harvest and in which must the seed now be sown for the first time.

As the science of missions (missiology) has developed, it has come to include a large number of subjects. Knowledge of other religions and other cultures, the history of missionary effort, the theological foundations of the Christian faith, expertise in the languages spoken, and on and on—all these are respectable parts of missiology.

There is grave danger, however, that these will come to be considered and taught as ends in themselves. This they must never be.

As these subjects are taught, their students must be urged to keep their eyes fixed upon the degree of discipling achieved in the specific population they are evangelizing.

Precisely the same thing must be emphasized in every seminary, Bible college, and ministerial gathering in the United States. The pastor must ask: Is my congregation growing? Ought it to be planting other congregations? The seminary professor must ask, Do our seminary courses prepare ministers who will multiply soundly Christian congregations in every great urbanization, every rural district, and every ethnic minority between the Gulf of Mexico and the North Pole? Every Bible school and seminary ought to conduct a survey of its graduates over the past twenty years and find out how many of them are winning the lost, planting new congregations, sending out missionaries, and praying ardently for the congregation to be effectively evangelistic. Every school of theological education could easily send out such a questionnaire to its graduates. Theological schools would then know how successful they had been in their attempts to graduate effective evangelists.

Denominational executives must know the growth patterns of all their congregations and which of them can be stimulated into much greater growth. We live in a highly secularized society. Unless we start seeing the real situation and carrying out effective evangelism as our God-given task, we shall be still further inundated by the secular, agnostic tide.

Conclusion

The tremendous spread of the church growth movement since 1961, when the Institute of Church Growth was founded in Eugene, Oregon, has been surprising to everyone.

The church growth movement on the one hand faced many slow-growing or declining denominations. It saw that the Christian faith was regarded by many as merely one of many religions in the world today. It observed with alarm that in too many Christian quarters the concept of a unified, brotherly world, was considered incompatible with a program of discipling segments of society. It observed tremendous numbers of static congregations and denominations.

As accurate pictures concerning church growth were collected from all over the world, it became apparent that only in some places church growth was occurring. It could and should occur in many more. If accurate knowledge of church growth were obtained, if schools of theological education and denominations were to take off the blindfolds and work in the light of facts, ripe fields could be reaped to the last sheaf.

God has been at work doing far more than anyone expected or thought possible. All of Africa south of the Sahara is in the process of becoming substantially Christian. Competent authorities tell us that there will be 357 million Christians in Africa by the year 2000. Since 1970 Christianity in China has expanded amazingly, principally because of the house church movement there. Vital Christianity is growing in the Philippines, Guatemala, Brazil, Korea, and many other lands.

Clearly we face the most receptive, responsive world ever to exist. If Christians of all nations will now press ahead obeying eternal God's command, we shall see tremendous church growth. If the Lord tarries, the number of Christians in the world will grow from one-fifth to perhaps one-half in the coming decades.

My pilgrimage has taken place in the midst of these tremendous divine movements. God has used the church growth movement far more than any of us laboring at it dared to ask or think.

7

Church Growth   1933–65

1933–36, Many Good Works, Static Memberships

The church growth movement began in the fourth decade of the twentieth century. During those years as field secretary of the India Mission I had the privilege to see not only my own mission but many other missionary efforts in various parts of the subcontinent of India. I found that all missions were engaged in good works. But only a few mission efforts were resulting in actual discipling of an *ethnos.* Too many national denominations and congregations were busy looking after themselves and caring only for existing Christians. Too many missions were maintaining as their chief or only work leprosy homes, feeding famine orphans, running mission schools, carrying on Christian medical work in dispensaries and hospitals, developing better methods of agriculture, and other similar good works. They were doing these many good works believing that as these were done, the Christian faith would spread.

However, the areas in which the Christian faith was actually spreading were few and far between. Often nine-tenths of a mission's resources were spent in doing good works, and less than one-tenth went to the actual spread of the Christian faith. Many congregations among the Methodists, Baptists, Presbyterians, Lutherans, Anglicans, and others continued on for years sometimes without adding a single non-Christian to the church. It became increasingly clear that something very much more effective ought to be instituted.

Just what this other program was, however, was not clear. World evangelization is a very complex process. It faces very different opportunities and difficulties as it evangelizes very different segments of humanity. All those who would obey eternal God's command to proclaim the gospel to all peoples, *leading them to faith and obedience,* must realize that many programs that achieve that end in one segment of society will not achieve that end in most other segments. Christian schools in many of the tribes of Africa have resulted in substantial Christianization. However, in most parts of vast India, China, and many other lands, Christian schools have seldom led to substantial Christianization.

During the fourth decade of this century as I faced these and similar facts, I was constantly asking the question, What then must we do? We pray the Lord of harvest to send laborers into whitened fields; but how must they reap these very different harvests? You do not reap potato fields with a sickle. Every crop presents certain significant differences.

1936–54, Eighteen Instructive Years

In 1936 my mission sent me to be the evangelistic missionary in the Takhatpur area, some three hundred villages spread across the plain around the small town of Takhatpur. In many of these villages lived ten to fifty families of Satnamis, a caste of a million, who had shown some appreciation for the gospel. My mission said to me, "We like your concern for effective evangelism. We will back your efforts to multiply churches in different areas. We will ask our supporting board to raise $25,000 to undergird a new and vigorous program of evangelism. What that program is will depend very largely upon you. We hope that God will make it successful."

Those eighteen years, therefore, were spent in an evangelism that attempted to win enough families in a given village to enable the establishment of new congregations.

Had this attempt been made in 1920 instead of 1940, it would without question have brought ten thousand to fifty thousand people to Christian faith. However, in 1940 Mahatma Gandhi was proclaiming that the end of British rule was at hand and that the Untouchables were to be regarded as Harijans, or God's people. Consequently, the receptivity of the Untouchable Satnamis sharply declined.

Alas, Mr. Gandhi's kind words and some attractive political concessions did not change the oppression the Satnamis suffered.

His kind words did, however, lead many of them to refuse to become Christian. "Hinduism," they, alas, vainly imagined, "is going to treat us fairly. Why should we become Christians?" Nevertheless, the evangelistic effort did bring in fifteen new small congregations.

At the same time, faced with several hundred Christian children in the villages who were growing up illiterate, I was burdened with the need for Christian education. Furthermore, the preventable deaths of many Christians underscored the need for building and maintaining a Christian hospital at Takhatpur. The very great need for agricultural improvements of various sorts made it seem necessary to stress agricultural development. Thus, despite convictions to the contrary, I found myself engaging in many good works; true, I gave more attention to evangelism than most missionaries, but I found that the Christian program the situation needed had to include many undertakings that seemed to bear little relation to the spread of the church.

Nevertheless, these eighteen years, 1936–54, during which I frequently studied other missions also and wrote a monthly article for the *United Church Review* (a Presbyterian magazine) did enable a church growth point of view to be developed. Convictions formed in my mind as to what had to be done. Some of these convictions grew out of my successes; others were based on my failures. In 1953 I wrote the manuscript of *The Bridges of God*. This was later published by World Dominion Press in London and Friendship Press in New York. According to Dr. Frank Price, a Southern Presbyterian missionary to China who had become the librarian at the Missionary Research Library in New York, this became "the most read missionary book in 1956."

1955–60, Additional Insights

In 1954 Mrs. McGavran and I completed our fourth seven-year term in India and came home on furlough, intending to return to India in 1955. However, my board, the United Christian Missionary Society, impressed by the need to know its various mission fields more accurately, sent me to Puerto Rico,Thailand, Belgian Congo, the Philippines, Jamaica, and Orissa, India. In each of these I was to survey not only the work of my society, but, as far as possible, the work of Baptists, Methodists, Presbyterians, and other mission boards. The information I received from surveying these many boards in most continents of the world greatly helped me develop a world wide church growth point of view that spoke to the real situations in most mission fields.

In 1958, finding that most mission leaders were inclined to think that I spoke chiefly about people movements to Christ and had started calling me "People Movement McGavran," I wrote a second book, *How Churches Grow.* In it I never mentioned people movements. This was in order to emphasize that the essential task of all world evangelization was to carry out the commands concerning finding and folding the lost. These commands must be obeyed, especially in the rapidly growing and many-faceted cities of the world and the responsive populations. The essential work was the spread of the Christian faith. The absolute center of evangelization was *matheteusate panta ta ethne,* incorporating all the segments of society into Christ's body. *How Churches Grow,* published by World Dominion Press and Friendship Press (1959), enabled this view of missions to spread in the English-speaking world.

However, most seminaries and Bible colleges still paid very little attention to church growth or effective evangelism and missionary societies. "That," they held, "was the work of professional evangelists." Training in evangelism—despite its clear centrality to New Testament theology—was very seldom taught. When it was, it was usually an elective. Pastors and ministers care for their flocks. They do not search for lost sheep or reap ripe fields. This mistaken notion has been an essential part of the rationale back of theological education.

I spent the years 1954–55 as a research fellow of Yale Divinity School. During 1956–57 I continued to live in New Haven, Connecticut on the edge of the Divinity School campus. From 1957 through 1960 the United Christian Missionary Society appointed me to a new position—professor of missions of its College of Missions. My duties were to teach outgoing candidates of the United Christian

Missionary Society at the summer sessions of the College of Missions and during the other three quarters of the year become peripatetic professor of missions in the seminaries of the Christian Church, Disciples of Christ. Thus, I taught in the graduate seminary of Phillips University, Enid, Oklahoma; the Divinity School in Des Moines, Iowa; Christian Theological Seminary in Indianapolis; the College of the Bible, Lexington, Kentucky; the School of Religion, Berkeley, California; Bethany College, West Virginia; and Northwest Christian College, Eugene, Oregon.

Interspersed with these teaching assignments were the church growth researches in the countries already mentioned. These researches were to be of the major Protestant missions in those lands. For example, in Puerto Rico my researches included careful studies of the Baptist, Congregational, Methodist, Pentecostal, and Presbyterian missions and churches, as well as those of my own denomination.

During these years the theological and conceptual bases of effective evangelism (church growth) were enlarged. My statements concerning church growth were framed to fit the general Protestant mission picture. The fact that church growth thinking was so generally acceptable across the spectrum of Protestant denominations can be credited in large part to these years, which combined finding the facts in many lands and teaching these in five seminaries and five summer courses of the College of Missions. Unrecognized by me, God was preparing me to speak convincingly to the worldwide church about discipling *panta ta ethne.*

January 1961 to September 1965

In 1959 it became clear to me that the church growth point of view should not be limited to the congregations, seminaries, and missionary societies of the Christian churches. All missionary effort of all branches of the universal church needed to hear and obey God commanding them to do more effective multiplication of congregations of the redeemed among *panta ta ethne.* My researches proved to me that most missions in most lands were obtaining less growth—often *far* less growth—than they could. Too often missionaries were substituting care for the existing flock for finding lost sheep. Too often they were substituting good deeds for effective evangelism. Too many missionaries were serving one nongrowing congregation or a half dozen nongrowing congregations instead of multiplying congregations of new believers among the vast multitudes of unbelievers. Too many missionaries, fresh out of American seminaries, were teaching in third world seminaries and were preparing ministers for existing slow-growing congregations. The theological schools in which they taught had not a single course on effective evangelism.

As I pondered these things, it became clear to me that I ought to resign from the missionary society and start an institute of church growth. This would enroll career missionaries from many denominations. It would also vitalize the beginning churches in scores and eventually thousands of different areas on the globe.

When I told this to my good friend, the chief executive of the United Christian Missionary Society, he replied, "You really must rethink your position. It would be foolish of you, now that you are sixty-three years of age, to do any such thing. You have a secure position now with your own missionary society. You wear a thirty-five-year pin. You are one of our honored veterans. Stay with us."

However, feeling strongly that God was calling me to labors that would help advance effective evangelization in many branches of the church in many lands, I resolved to resign as a missionary of the United Christian Missionary Society and to found an institute of church growth.

I approached three of the Christian Church seminaries and asked that they start institutes of church growth. All of them declined, saying that it was a good idea, but they did not have the money. In the spring of 1959, while serving as professor of missions in Northwest Christian College for a quarter, I mentioned my dream to President Ross Griffeth. He replied, "We would be happy to have you as a member of our faculty. You could begin the Institute of Church Growth here. All the college would require would be for you to teach one course on missions every quarter to our undergraduates. The rest of your time you could spend teaching the career missionaries from many denominations attending the Institute of

Church Growth. Furthermore, we will be glad to give three $1,000 scholarships to career missionaries of any denomination who would come here to study church growth."

A small Christian college in far-off Eugene, Oregon, was not the best place to start an institute of church growth. However, since it was the only possible place, I decided to accept President Griffeth's offer.

In the school year 1959–60 the United Christian Missionary Society sent me to teach missions in Bethany College, West Virginia, and in the fall of 1960 to be professor of missions in the School of Religion on Holy Hill in Berkeley, California, right next to the University of California. The School of Religion there had written over the doorway to its chapel, "Go into all the world and preach the gospel." The Congregational Seminary, when it built that chapel, had been ardently missionary, but by the fall of 1960 it had become cold toward missions, and my classes there were small. The main concern of the seminary was not effective evangelism.

In mid-December 1960 our term of service at the School of Religion ended. We packed our belongings into our small trailer, covered them with a tarpaulin, hitched the trailer to our car, and drove six hundred miles north to Eugene, Oregon, to establish the Institute of Church Growth.

The first classes of the Institute of Church Growth opened on January 2, 1961 with one student, the Rev. Keith Hamilton of the Methodist Mission in Bolivia. For the next five months he was my sole student. I had the unrivaled opportunity of forming the courses of instruction of the Institute of Church Growth before a very small audience. However, his researches into the Christianization of the Aymara and Quechua Indian tribes of the high Andes gave me an opportunity to become well acquainted with what was happening in all the nations of western South America—Colombia, Ecuador, Peru, Bolivia, and Chile. It was a most rewarding five months.

In the fall the number of students increased. The courses of study that I had roughly outlined in the spring of that year were expanded and taught again. It was cheering to note that the career missionaries all felt that their courses of study were distinctly helpful to them. Their researches also into what had actually happened in six different mission fields were most illuminating. These researches abundantly justified the church growth point of view.

Because of the small enrollment, President Griffeth said to me, "Rather than tying up one of our classrooms, I think that you had better hold your classes in that part of the library where we stack the books yet to be catalogued. There in the stacks you will find a large and beautiful oak table, around which ten students can easily sit. If you stand at one end and lecture, your classes will be held in a very quiet part of the college." Consequently, for the next four and a half years all the classes of the Institute of Church Growth were held around that oak table in the stacks.

The Rev. Alan Tippett arrived in late December of 1961. He was a twenty-year veteran Australian Methodist missionary to the Fiji Islands. I had granted him a $1,000 research fellowship, because I liked what he wrote in the *International Review of Missions* about the spread of Christianity in the Pacific Islands. He liked the emphasis of the classes in the Institute of Church Growth. In the spring of 1962 I said to him, "Alan, how about your teaching two two-hour courses, one on animism (which you know very well from your twenty years' work among the animists of Fiji) and one on anthropology? The courses you are taking in anthropology in the University of Oregon across the street and your experience amply qualify you to do this."

Since he needed the additional income, he gladly accepted. The Institute of Church Growth now had two teachers—Alan Tippett, who taught four hours a week, and Donald McGavran, who taught twelve.

In the first week of September, 1961, the annual meeting of the Evangelical Foreign Missions Association, headed by Dr. Clyde Taylor, was held in Winona Lake, Indiana. Dr. Taylor invited me to deliver a series of lectures on church growth to that meeting. The executive secretaries assembled there liked what they heard.They said, "This kind of instruction should be given to all our missionaries on furlough. Would you be willing to come here next year at this same time and speak to a gathering of possibly a hundred career missionaries on furlough? We will pay your way to and from Eugene. Edwin Jacques, executive secretary for the Conservative Baptists, will manage the seminar. All you have to do is lecture on church growth."

Thus the annual Seminar on Church Growth at Winona Lake was born. Every year for the next nine years EFMA missionaries and many others on furlough assembled at Winona Lake for four days of instruction in church growth. What later was published as *Understanding Church Growth* formed the subject matter of these lectures. For the first four years the only lecturer was Donald McGavran. After that time the program was enriched by lectures from Ralph Winter, Alan Tippett, and others.

This Church Growth Seminar, attended by more than one thousand career missionaries over the years, had a considerable impact on mission thinking.

The Congress on the Church's Worldwide Mission at Wheaton, Illinois, in 1966 had a section on church growth, the first time church growth as a distinct topic had been assigned an important place in mission theory.

Year by year as enrolled career missionaries from all over the world studied at the Institute of Church Growth and researched the actual growth of the church in their fields, some of the exact information needed by world evangelization was being gathered. In 1962–63 one research fellow came from Nigeria, one from Brazil, and another from South Korea. Three brilliant church growth researches resulted. For the first time, what church growth had actually happened in each of those places was described. Roy Shearer's graphs showed that the districts in the central and southern part of Korea, now the Republic of Korea, had shown moderate or small growth while the two districts in north Korea, now Communist North Korea, just south of the Yalu River had shown tremendous growth. As Shearer explored why missionary labors had had these distinctly different results in different parts of the country, he cast a great deal of new light on what had actually happened. His exact thinking burst through the promotional language employed by most exponents of mission. A brilliant new light was shed on where and how evangelism was being effective and where and why it was not.

The same was true of William Read's work on church growth in Brazil and of Gordon Robinson's and John Grimley's work on church growth in Nigeria. All three of these researches were later published under the titles, *Wildfire—Church Growth in Korea, New Patterns of*

Church Growth in Brazil, and *Church Growth in Central and Southern Nigeria.*

During the four and a half years, forty-three researches were completed. Dependable information on actual church growth in many lands was assembled. The victories and defeats were set forth in meaningful detail. What causes church growth and what causes static, nongrowing congregations became increasingly clear. None of these researches, however, was published in America before 1966. The Institute of Church Growth did not have the money or the prestige. However, *Church Growth in the High Andes* by Keith Hamilton and *Church Growth in Jamaica* by McGavran were published in India by the Lucknow Press before 1965. The others were not published until 1966–67. Indeed, most of the forty-three were never published.

The Annual Church Growth Lectures at Eugene also nurtured and furthered the church growth movement. Noted mission executives and missionaries were invited to address the institute on the subject of church growth. Their lectures were then published (after 1965). Bishop J. Waskom Pickett gave the first lectures. In the second set of lectures in the fall of 1963, Dr. Eugene Nida (American Bible Society), Dr. Cal Guy (Southwest Baptist Theological Seminary), the Rev. Melvin Hodges (executive secretary for Latin America, Foreign Missions Department, Assemblies of God, Springfield, Missouri), and I delivered the twelve lectures. The audience included more than twenty mission executives from many of the mission boards in North America, as well as the career missionaries attending the institute. These influential lectures were published in 1965 by Harper and Row under the title *Church Growth and Christian Mission.* The book has made a notable contribution to the church growth movement.

In 1963 the World Council of Churches assembled a large world gathering in Montreal, Canada. One part of their program, led by the celebrated Victor Hayward, Baptist mission executive from England, was a study of the church growth movement. This was ample evidence of the wide effect the church growth movement was having, even back in 1963. The church growth conference was attended by about twenty representatives who came from all six continents. I was invited to explain and defend the church growth position. I wrote back to Victor Hayward immediately asking whether he would also include Bishop J. Waskom Pickett of the United Methodist Church and the Rev. Alan Tippett, my associate teacher at the Institute of Church Growth. He answered with a cordial yes.

The church growth conference was assembled at Iberville, a small town near Montreal. The findings were known as "The Growth of the Church, a Statement Drawn up by a Special Consultation Convened by the WCC Department of Missionary Studies at Iberville, Quebec, July 31–August 2, 1963."

For the first two days of the conference church growth was subjected to sustained attacks voiced chiefly by Victor Hayward. Instead of answering these myself, I urged Bishop Pickett and Mr. Tippett to defend church growth. On occasion I also explained and described what church growth really meant. It threatened nothing in essential Christianity. It furthered the basic concerns of the propagation of the gospel. At the end of the second day Pickett, Tippett, and I felt sure that the findings of this conference would be a critical assessment of the church growth movement.

Between the second and third day Victor Hayward took the evening and possibly much of the night to write up a considered statement on church growth, which he read out to the conference the next day for debate and decision. I was delighted. It was an open, well-stated, reasoned description of the church growth movement. There was little debate—a few words here and there were changed. The conference called by the World Council of Churches had enthusiastically backed church growth.

However, instead of publishing this report in the *International Review of Missions,* the World Council published it in the *Ecumenical Review* and never thereafter mentioned it. Nevertheless, the Institute of Church Growth and later the School of World Mission at Fuller Theological Seminary found this statement an excellent exposition of the whole church growth position. We published and republished it many times. Thousands of copies were printed and mailed out with personal letters. Copies were sent to all those considering coming to us to study missions. The Iberville report had a considerable impact. It was not our statement. It was a statement of a conference of the World Council of Churches. It had a great impact on the evangelical wing of the universal church. The conciliar wing, moving steadily away from evangelism toward social action, paid little attention to it.

In June 1964, as soon as he had received his doctoral degree in anthropology from the University of Oregon, Alan Tippett left for the South Pacific. He had been teaching at the Institute of Church Growth for two and a quarter years. Since the financial ability of the Institute of Church Growth to engage a second full-time teacher was nonexistent, I never expected to see him again. Tippett's place as teacher of animism and anthropology was taken by the Rev. George Martindale, a Conservative Baptist missionary to Japan on furlough, and the program of instruction at the Institute of Church Growth proceeded steadily onward for the academic year 1964–65. His services ended in June of 1965 when, as described in the next chapter, the Institute of Church Growth became the School of World Mission at Fuller Theological Seminary in southern California.

A most significant development occurred in 1964. The Rev. Norman Cummings, the director of administration for Overseas Crusades, a large missionary society founded about 1950, had sent a number of his missionaries on furlough to the Institute of Church Growth. In the spring of 1964 he himself came to study for a month. Toward the end of his stay he said to me, "Dr. McGavran, this institute should have a publication. What you are saying needs to be read by thousands of people."

I replied, "I thoroughly agree. But we do not have the money."

He responded, "If you will provide the copy, Overseas Crusades will provide the funds for printing and mailing. We will also secure a mailing list of several thousand."

Consequently, in October of 1964 the first issue of the *Church Growth Bulletin* came out. It has been published ever since then every two months. It has called attention around the world to the importance and urgency of effective evangelism. It has influenced scores of missionary societies and has carried articles by many of the leaders of world mission today. In the early eighties its title was changed to *Global Church Growth*. In 1987 Overseas Crusades ceased publishing it, and its publisher became the Church Growth Center at Corunna, Indiana. Dr. Kent Hunter became editor-in-chief.

Every four or five years the publications have been bound into a volume on church growth. These volumes are probably the best source for detailed description of church growth in every continent. The world of missions owes a great debt to Norman Cummings and Overseas Crusades and now Dr. Kent Hunter.

In 1964, as a result of the researches done by career missionaries from Latin America, I came to feel that a scientific, on-the-spot research into church growth in all the Latin American lands would be a major contribution to mission thinking and planning. In consequence, I wrote to twenty foundations asking for grants to fund the proposed church growth survey, which would cover all of South America. Nineteen of my proposals proved fruitless, but the twentieth, addressed to the Eli Lilly Endowment of Indianapolis, bore fruit. One day in December of 1964 I received a check for $54,000, and the Latin American church growth project was born.

In the spring of 1965, after much correspondence, three career missionary researchers were secured. William Read of the Presbyterian Mission in Brazil, Harmon Johnson of the Assemblies of God, and Victor Monterroso, a Baptist minister and seminary lecturer in Costa Rica, were selected as the three researchers. Scheduled to begin work in September of 1965, they were to assemble at the Institute of Church Growth in Oregon for several months of book research before fanning out to the various lands in the great continent to the south. Since in June of 1965 Northwest Christian College decided to terminate the Institute of Church Growth, I decided to accept Fuller Theological Seminary's invitation to become the founding dean of its new School of World Mission.

Therefore, in September of 1965 the three men assembled in Pasadena, California, rather than Eugene, Oregon. Their researches during the next two years resulted in a notable contribution to the cause of missions, the book *Latin American Church Growth*. They did careful church growth researches in seventeen Latin American nations. For the first time those carrying on mission in all those countries saw from graphs of growth and columns of statistics what church growth had actually been achieved. Pages of description told why some missionary efforts had succeeded greatly and why many others had established a few small nongrowing congregations. The whole enterprise was a notable contribution both to missiology, the science, and to the carrying out of the Great Commission. It carried one step further the series of forty-three researches done by career missionaries who studied at the Institute of Church Growth.

Hence, while it was carried out very largely by the School of World Mission in Pasadena, the account of the Latin American church growth project is included in the section of this book describing the Institute of Church Growth. Such researches need to be carried out from decade to decade so that world evangelization remains well informed as to what measures and methods God is blessing, to the growth of the church, and what He is not blessing.

Jim Sunda, an Alliance missionary, studied at the Institute of Church Growth in 1964. He described the very remarkable discipling of thousands of West Danis in the western half of the great island of New Guinea. Since his was a most dramatic story and a wonderful example of large discipling, I sent his manuscript to India to be published by the Lucknow Press. His was a notable contribution to the science of missiology.

All such information is also an essential part of theological education. Unless pastors in preparation see an accurate picture of the degree to which the people in their cities or counties are practicing Christians, nominal Christians, or non-Christians, they cannot win many through conversion to Christian faith. Unless theological schools also see these things accurately for their own and other nations, they cannot know what eternal God's command to disciple the peoples of earth means to church leaders today.

Thus, at the Institute of Church Growth between January of 1961 and June of 1965 many notable contributions to church growth thinking were made. Year by year leaders of the universal church had impressed upon them that the actual winning of men and women to Christ and the multiplication of congregations, far from being the concern only of missionary societies and professional evangelists, were the concern of the entire church. Seminary professors, mission executives, and all leaders of all denominations needed to know what was actually happening in regard to the discipling of the unsaved in their own nations and in all other nations. It was not enough to shepherd existing churches and proclaim the gospel widely. The goal was much more than that. The goal was to multiply sound, believing, Spirit-filled congregations in every segment of society in North America and the other five continents as well. The degree to which this goal was being achieved needed constantly to be accurately measured and made the basis for future action. *This is the central business of all missiology, of all courses on evangelism, and, indeed, of all theological education.*

The brief four and a half years of church growth thinking, teaching, research, and publishing of the Institute of Church Growth at Northwest Christian College had been greatly blessed by God.

8

Church Growth   1965–71

Effective Evangelism—the Heart of Missiology

Charles Fuller, whose vision and money have so greatly furthered the evangelical Christian enterprise, wanted in 1944 to establish a school of world mission. He himself, in his radio broadcasts of "The Old Fashioned Revival Hour," was carrying out effective radio evangelization across America. But he longed to obey Christ's command to enroll all the peoples of the earth in the church of Christ (Matt. 28:19).

As he sought to implement this vision, he established as a first step a theological seminary. Fuller Theological Seminary held its first classes in 1946 in Pasadena, California. It soon became one of the outstanding evangelical seminaries in North America. By 1963, of its eight hundred graduates, two hundred had gone abroad as missionaries.

In that year, when David Hubbard was called to the presidency of the seminary, he and Charles Fuller decided that the time had come to establish a second graduate school. This would deal with world evangelization. It would be called the School of World Mission and have a faculty of seven full-time academically and experientially qualified professors.

As a part of this vision and this planning, the seminary wrote to its two hundred graduates who were missionaries in many parts of the world and asked, "Whom should we call as dean of this new school of world mission?" More than half of their replies suggested that they look into a man called Donald McGavran. "He," they said, "is saying some very important and very timely things about Christian mission." All this was completely unknown to me.

One day in February of 1965, as I was teaching a class of six career

79

missionaries seated around the oak table in the library stacks at Northwest Christian College, a couple of distinguished-looking men walked into the classroom and asked if they could join the class and listen to the teaching. I assured them that they were most welcome. At the end of the class they asked, "Are you going to teach another class this morning?"

I assured them that I was and that they were very welcome to visit it also. They introduced themselves to me as David Hubbard, president of Fuller Theological Seminary, and C. Davis Weyerhaeuser, chairman of the seminary board. At the close of the second class they said, "We are now going out to lunch but would like to come back about two o'clock and have some further conversation." I assured them that I would be pleased to talk with them. At the two-o'clock meeting they told me that they were looking for a dean for the new school of mission shortly to be established at Fuller Theological Seminary in Pasadena. They were considering me for the appointment. Would I be willing to come down and talk to the faculty?

At the same time, President Ross Griffeth had reached the age of sixty-eight, and a new president of Northwest Christian College was being called. I was also going to be sixty-eight in 1965 and asked the board whether it would continue my services and the Institute of Church Growth. Much consultation resulted. The fact that a $54,000 grant had been received from the Eli Lilly Endowment to carry on the Latin American Church Growth project was a point of interest. The new president of the college did not feel that he wanted to carry on the Institute of Church Growth. A majority of his board, however, were in favor of continuing it.

After much discussion the board decided in 1965 to discontinue the Institute of Church Growth at Northwest Christian College. Consequently, I went to Fuller Theological Seminary as the founding dean of its School of World Mission.

That summer, by previous arrangement, I spent two months in Brazil giving courses on church growth at three Presbyterian seminaries in southern, central, and northern Brazil. When I returned, I came not to Eugene but to Pasadena, where, during my absence in Brazil, Mrs. McGavran had moved our household goods and books.

In June, 1965, President Hubbard had asked me to secure a second member of the faculty of the School of World Mission. He had agreed with my recommendation that this man be Dr. Alan Tippett. He joined the School of World Mission on the day it began in late September.

The fifteen career missionaries who formed the student body had all intended to come to Eugene and were pleased that instead they were coming to the School of World Mission of Fuller Theological Seminary at Pasadena.

While the School of World Mission was a graduate institution separate from the School of Theology, during that first year when we had only two teachers (Tippett and myself), it was difficult for the professors in the theological school to think of us as other than a department of the seminary. Nevertheless, President Hubbard stoutly maintained that we were a separate graduate school. Students who enrolled in the School of World Mission took all their courses in the School of World Mission and worked toward a graduate degree in missions. All the administration of the School of World Mission took place in faculty meetings attended only by Tippett and McGavran.

This gave the new school great opportunity to develop courses of study that met the real needs of world evangelization carried on by hundreds of missionary societies in Asia, Africa, Latin America, and the islands of the seas.

The following courses were given in 1965–66: the underlying principles of church growth, hidden psychological and cultural factors that arrest growth, how pastoral training can promote (or prevent) church growth, understanding and measuring church growth, animism and church growth, theology and church growth, and anthropology and missions.

The School of World Mission used the sciences of man, such as sociology and anthropology, to increase understanding of the complex and little-known processes of church growth out of non-Christian populations. In training missionaries these sciences have often been used to reduce the Westerner's ethnocentrism—his smug sense of superiority. The School of World Mission did not use these sciences that way. It used them to obtain more and better church growth, that men may be reconciled to God. Case studies of specific younger churches enabled our career missionaries to see how church and mission policies, methods, and attitudes encourage or block reconciling men to God.

In planning the curriculum for this significant first year of the School of World Mission, I held that those responsible for carrying out Christian mission and making important decisions concerning its processes should take training in church growth. Failure on the part of mission executives and missionaries themselves to make right decisions many times defeats the basic purpose of world evangelization. Ignorance of church growth principles makes leaders susceptible to wrong decisions in planning and carrying out missions. Those in charge of carrying out effective worldwide evangelization should be obeying eternal God's command to proclaim the gospel to all peoples, leading them to faith and obedience. Consequently, they must see winning men and women to Christ and multiplying churches as the one true purpose of mission. In short, field directors, district superintendents, church and mission executives, and others in places of responsibility must see church growth as the heart of all Christian mission. This was the purpose of the School of World Mission as it began its work in Pasadena, California. The School of World Mission had incorporated the Institute of Church Growth into its fundamental being.

A significant part of the work of the School of World Mission that first year was directing the Latin American Church growth research. This involved travel by team members to Latin America, long detailed reports about church growth in its many missions, decisions as to what additional information had to be acquired, many sessions reviewing, editing, and amplifying the findings of the three members of the research team, and special classes for them in addition to the classes for the career missionaries.

Choosing a Faculty

President Hubbard had instructed me to recruit one full-time professor of missions in each of the following years. A considerable part of the work was, therefore, numerous interviews with men who

I thought might be good additions to our faculty.

We wanted the faculty to be men who thoroughly agreed that the heart of missions was not merely doing good works and preaching the gospel in every land and every city, but also and most importantly discipling segment after segment of mankind. This meant multiplying sound, Bible-believing, Spirit-filled congregations whose members were made up of converts from Islam, Hinduism, Buddhism, animism, Confucianism, and nominal Christianity.

The term "missiology" was not then commonly used. Instead we talked about the science of missions, about courses that a school of world mission ought to teach. The science of missions is a very complex subject. The missionary must know and speak well the language of the people whom he evangelizes. He must be well aware of their religion and what they believe. He must be well acquainted with their culture and what they consider desirable and undesirable. He should be well instructed in previous missionary efforts in that land among those peoples—tribes, classes, castes, and other segments of society. He should also have a thorough knowledge of the major missionary concerns of the Bible. He should sincerely believe that if one is to be a biblically sound Christian, he must aim at effective world evangelization at home and abroad. There is no other way to carry out Christ's commands than to disciple all the peoples of the world. Steps must be taken so that the day may speedily dawn when "every knee should bow . . . and every tongue confess that Jesus Christ is Lord" (Phil. 2:10-11). The science of missions is a complex science.

Since every missionary can carry on his work in a far distant land only as he is supported by fellow Christians in his own native land, he must know how to present to his supporters the cause of world evangelization most effectively. He must be able to raise his salary from people to whom he speaks for maybe thirty minutes. In short, he must be an able promoter. *However, he must not carry on his work in the light of his promotional addresses.* He must carry on his work in the light of the actual conditions and the actual progress of his program of evangelization.

Every missionary sits in two chairs—one, the promotional chair when he is communicating his efforts to his supporters; the second, the diagnostic chair. When sitting on the latter chair he is representing the exact situation to his Lord. He must always plan his future and determine what he actually does from day to day in the light of his reports while sitting on the diagnostic chair. He must constantly plan his work in the light of what is actually happening by way of discipling all that *ethnos* to which the Lord has sent him.

The recruitment of the faculty would have to take place from among those experienced missionaries who were prepared to teach some aspect of the science of mission while adhering firmly to the belief that the success of their labors must always be measured by the number of sheaves they were bringing in.

This severely limited the choice of professors. As missionaries go out around the world, some of them become engaged in educational work, and some in medical work; some are teachers in theological seminaries, and some are preaching the gospel in highly resistant segments of the population where many hear but few become baptized followers of the Lord Jesus. Furthermore, some are heavily influenced by courses in comparative religions and anthropology. Unfortunately, some of them believe that knowing these subjects is important to the missionary whether he ever multiplies congregations or not.

Schools of mission are in constant danger of recruiting faculties from missionaries who have done little by way of planting churches or who hold vigorously to the position that the church needs not to be expanded but purged; that, far from doubling, it must be halved; and that only then does it become pure, holy, consecrated—the true church. Such scholars were not going to be asked to become our faculty members.

The next two men invited to become members of the faculty were Edwin Orr, a Ph.D. from Oxford University in England and noted evangelist, and Ralph Winter, a Ph.D. from Cornell University, serving as a Presbyterian missionary in Guatemala among the Quiche Indians. I chose Edwin Orr because, while he had not been a missionary in some non-Christian land, he did have a passion for winning men to Christ. He was also keenly aware that the Bible requires such a concern as a part of the normal Christian life. He was sure that winning to Christian faith enormous numbers of the lost in

America, Europe, and every land was part of normal Christian life.

I called Dr. Winter to the faculty partly because a single sentence in one of his writings had attracted my attention. He had written, "Much more important than all the gimmicks and gadgets of missionary life is bringing men and women into accountable fellowship in the local church." Furthermore, he would bring to the faculty someone concerned with the vast Latin American field.

The faculty obviously needed someone from Africa. Quite a number of career missionaries from Africa had studied at the Institute of Church Growth and the School of World Mission in Pasadena in the years 1961–68. Opportunities for church growth in the huge land mass which is Africa south of the Sahara Desert had been borne in on me by their researches and by my 1954 journey across Africa.

When I had traveled across Africa in 1954 from Nairobi to Accra, I had formed the conviction that by the year 2000 there would be at least 100 million Christians in Africa south of the Sahara. While this view had been laughed at by African missionary authorities in New York, it was abundantly confirmed by Dr. David Barrett, whom I invited to lecture at our school in 1968. Indeed, he insisted that 100 million was far too small a figure. I asked him to elaborate his ideas, and he sent me an article for the *Church Growth Bulletin*, which was published in May of 1969. In it he stated that by the year 2000 there would be at least 350 million Christians in Africa. Later this article was republished in the *International Review of Missions* and parts of it in *Time* magazine.

Obviously, Africa was a very important mission field. More than six thousand Protestant missionaries were working in its various nations. Any school of missions must have a man from Africa. Furthermore, Dr. Tippett's strong points were his extensive knowledge of anthropology and animism. "Let Dr. Tippett continue his courses on animism," I said, "while we get a new professor who knows both Africa and anthropology." In 1969 I called to the faculty Dr. Charles Kraft. His experience in missions had been in Nigeria, in the southern and central parts of which Christianity had made great progress. In my estimation the southern two-thirds of the country would become solidly Christian in a few decades.

The next professor on the faculty obviously had to be someone

from east Asia. This enormous land mass comprising many nations—
Japan, Korea, Taiwan, China, Vietnam, Cambodia, and Thailand—
had in 1969 a population of well over one billion souls. Christianiz-
ing these vast populations was obviously a very large part of Christian mission. The School of World Mission needed somebody who
knew these nations well. To them were going and would go a large
number of career missionaries. At just this time Dr. Arthur Glasser,
home secretary of China Inland Mission (now called Overseas Missionary Fellowship), was resigning from that position. I had heard
him speak at the Wheaton Congress on the Church's Worldwide
Mission and had been impressed. His own experience in China in
1946–48 had been brief, but since then he had traveled widely in east
Asia and other parts of the world and knew missions from the
viewpoint of a most successful executive of a great missionary
society. Since he was obviously the best man available and personal
conversation confirmed that he thoroughly agreed with the School
of World Mission's basic convictions about effective evangelism, I
invited him to become a member of the faculty, and he came in
September of 1970. Mrs. McGavran invited the Glassers to be our
guests at 1430 Morada Place until they found a suitable house to rent.

In 1970 I turned seventy-three years of age and felt that the time
had come to appoint a new dean of the School of World Mission.
Arthur Glasser, home secretary of a great missionary society, would
obviously make a good dean. However, when he came, he asked that
he spend the first year here as one of the teachers. Consequently, he
became dean on July 1, 1971. On the same date I became dean
emeritus and a full-time professor for the next several years.

One of the career missionaries studying at the School of World
Mission in the late sixties had been C. Peter Wagner. He was a
missionary of the Andes Evangelical Mission in the great city of La
Paz. During his year of study here, I had been impressed with his
great ability and sound views on Christian mission. Furthermore, it
became increasingly clear that Latin America south of Panama was
quite a different part of the globe than the countries of Central
America from Panama to Mexico, which Dr. Winter knew so well.
The faculty of the School of World Mission needed someone from
one of the following countries: Brazil, Argentina, Paraguay, Chile,

Bolivia, Peru, Ecuador, Colombia, Venezuela. A number of possibilities presented themselves to my mind. I had had men from most of these countries studying with me. From among them all, however, I chose Peter Wagner, whose concern for bringing in the sheaves had impressed me. He did not have a doctoral degree; but I was sure he could easily earn one during the first few years of his professorship. I called him to the faculty in 1971. The faculty of seven full-time members was now complete.

Accurate Portrayal of the Degree of Church Growth

In addition to emphasizing effective evangelism and building up the faculty, the School of World Mission needed to assemble accurate information on what missions and the denominations planted by them in more than one hundred lands were actually achieving by way of discipling *panta ta ethne*. It was too easy and most dangerous to assume in promotional fashion that the world was now covered by missionaries and "great national churches." It was entirely erroneous to conclude that the work of missions was now substantially completed. Accurate pictures of the state of the churches in all lands were desperately needed. Were they growing, or were they static? Had half or more of the population become Christian, or did the Christians number one-tenth of one percent? Among the many segments of which the population in each nation was composed, in how many had effective evangelism been carried out and in how many had it not? Which were the fields white to harvest and in which fields was it necessary to throw out the stones before the land could even be plowed, let alone sown?

The master's and doctoral theses, which all students at the School of World Mission completed as an essential part of their studies, described, tabulated, and set forth precisely this type of information. Each thesis was supposed to supply authoritative answers to these questions. Nothing like this had ever been done in schools of missions before. Too many books on mission spent 250 pages describing other aspects of the missionary task. Then they devoted only two or three pages—or perhaps two or three paragraphs—to this heart of Christian mission.

Consequently, at the School of World Mission year by year theses describing accurately the outcome of Christian mission were completed and bound. Those relating to the outcome of mission in Latin America were bound in green. Asian researches were bound in red, African in blue, and those dealing with the theology and theoretical aspects of the situation, in black. By 1986 five shelves, twelve feet long, on the north wall of the public hall at the School of World mission were filled with more than six hundred researches done in the past twenty-one years. A flood of light has been poured on the effectiveness of the missionary enterprise in hundreds of mission fields. It is no longer necessary to work in the dark. Those concerned with world evangelization can now know what aspects of effective evangelization they need to stress.

As a result of these studies and this emphasis, it became increasingly clear that despite the eight thousand missionaries and many strong national denominations at work in Africa, considerable numbers of African tribes were as yet undiscipled. The Christians among these animists were men and women of other tribes that had become Christian but who, for various reasons, were now living in a tribe not their own.

The same was true of every continent, including North America. The Jews in North America, for example, are an unreached people. So are the Muslims and the Hindus in North America. So are the million Portuguese immigrants living largely between Philadelphia and Boston.

Dr. Winter prepared an extensive series of maps showing the enormous number of unreached peoples in various parts of the world. Ed Dayton of World Vision published a series of books on the unreached peoples, segments of society. Some missiologists state that there are now seventeen thousand unreached peoples. Others maintain that there are at least one hundred thousand. Both are correct, depending on the definition of an unreached people. This emphasis on locating the unreached peoples of the world and portraying accurately how each is being discipled is one of the notable contributions of the School of World Mission to missiology.

During the years 1965-72 a great many researches were carried out in various parts of the world by members of the School of World

Mission faculty. How effective is the Christian mission in this segment of society? How many churches have in fact been established? Are they multiplying? Do societies of the redeemed, as part of their redemption, establish other societies? Where are younger churches growing? Where are they disastrously static? Why are some growing? Why are some not growing? Researches in many lands by members of the faculty and students constantly spoke to these questions.

Other Significant Advances in Effective Evangelism

The annual Church Growth Seminar at Winona Lake was duplicated at Biola College in southern California and continued for several years. It drew in hundreds who could not have gone to far-off Indiana.

Graduates of the School of World Mission returning to their fields also carried out effective church growth researches in these fields. Space will not permit an enumeration of the many fields thus explored. One must suffice. A nationwide survey of church growth in the Philippines was instituted. In the fall of 1968 Leonard Tuggy of the Conservative Baptists and Ralph Toliver of the Overseas Missionary Fellowship, after studying at the School of World Mission for a year, returned to the Philippines to carry out a survey of church growth in those beautiful islands. Their book, *See the Church in the Philippines*, was published in 1972.

A vast curiosity had been aroused by the church growth movement as to what was really happening. It was felt increasingly urgent that the hard realities behind the flowery promotional presentation must be seen if mission was to be intelligent, if God's plan for the salvation of the world was to be carried out. An accurate picture of the rising clusters of congregations and denominations must be presented. A true account of whether younger churches were in fact discipling the unreached *ethne* round about them or—as was too often true—were not doing anything significant along that line, had to become a regular part of worldwide evangelism.

A concern for church growth—effective evangelism—was being aroused in denomination after denomination, in seminary after seminary, and in Bible college after Bible college. An elective two-hour course on evangelism was seen to be totally inadequate.

Books on church growth started to proliferate. Among these, *Understanding Church Growth* was one of the most widely read. Published studies on church growth in Korea, Africa, the Philippines, India, and many other lands were appearing with increasing frequency.

The American Society of Missiology

The Association of Professors of Missions held its meeting in Scarritt College, Nashville, Tennessee in 1972. I had been invited to deliver four lectures on church growth to this body. Church growth was to be the program. I accepted the invitation, requesting only that my contribution be limited to two lectures and that Dr. Glasser, the new dean of the school, and Dr. Wagner also speak. Consequently, that meeting included the following four lectures:

- "What Is the Church Growth School of Thought?" by Donald McGavran
- "Church Growth Theology" by Arthur F. Glasser
- "Missiological Research in the Fuller Seminary School of Mission" by C. Peter Wagner
- "The Homogeneous Unit in Mission Theory" by Donald McGavran

These lectures on the modern science of missions further encouraged the gathering to use the word "missiology" instead of "missions" or the "science of missions." Just as the science of the earth was geology, so the science of missions was missiology. The American Society of Missiology, ASM, was formed. It publishes an influential magazine, *Missiology*, and has had a marked impact upon the missionary enterprise. Dr. Alan Tippett became its most influential first editor, and Dr. Arthur Glasser its second.

Because members of ASM came from evangelical missionary societies, liberal missionary societies, and Roman Catholic missionary societies, some evangelicals questioned whether such a mixture would voice thoroughly biblical convictions on missiology. In answer it was argued that since evangelicals would constitute the majority in the society, they could assure that outcome. However, with the passing of the years, many evangelicals felt it necessary to convene an annual meeting of their own missiologists and called themselves the Association of Evangelical Professors of Mission.

The years 1965–71 were a most significant step in preparing men and women to carry out God's command to effectively evangelize the world. This chapter has dealt with some of the major movements of those six years. It cannot begin to describe all of them. The graduates of the School of World Mission during those six years in many cases became the leaders of missionary societies and began influencing mission and church policies in many parts of the world. The driving forces that had controlled the missionary enterprise in the early days and had been diminishing after World War II began to be reactivated. A new day for effective evangelism began to dawn.

9

Church Growth   1971–85

American Church Growth Is Born

Until 1971 the church growth movement had been concerned very largely with overseas missions. My own experience as an overseas missionary and the fact that the movement was developing in a school of world mission guaranteed that. True, there had been frequent references to the fact that the principles of church growth also applied to "Christianized" lands like the United States and Europe. In 1966 and 1967 the Rev. Medford Jones, a noted evangelist, tried, at my invitation, to make the Winona Lake annual Church Growth Seminar a meeting place for ministers of many denominations whose congregations were in the United States. They attended lectures by Mr. Jones and most of mine. Nevertheless, church growth and the *Church Growth Bulletin* were devoted overwhelmingly to the work of foreign missions.

As long as four-fifths or more of the world's population remains non-Christian, and Asia and North Africa remain overwhelmingly non-Christian, all schools of mission will, beyond doubt, spend most of their time on discipling the non-Christian *ethne* of Asia, Africa, and Latin America. Beginning in 1972, however, effective evangelism in the United States and other "Christian" lands began to be taken seriously by the church growth movement.

In 1972 Professor C. Peter Wagner, believing that church growth needed to be promoted in North America, told me he was planning to gather a group of thirty ministers and laymen of congregations in or near Pasadena for an accredited seminary course on church growth. Every Tuesday morning there would be one three-hour class session held at the Lake Avenue Congregational Church from

7 to 10 o'clock. He and I would share the teaching load. I gladly assented to his proposal.

As these ministers saw what church growth would mean in southern California and the United States as a whole, they became increasingly enthusiastic. Dr. Wagner resolved to have other similar accredited classes for American ministers.

One of the men enrolled in this course was Dr. Winfield Arn, who was at that time director of Christian education for the Evangelical Covenant Church in California, Arizona, and Nevada. As Dr. Arn listened with amazement and understanding to the church growth point of view, he resolved to start the Institute for American Church Growth. When he came to tell me of his plan, I cautioned him, saying, "Win, at your age you had better not resign from your secure post to start a new enterprise. You may lose your shirt." Disregarding my advice, he resigned his well-paying position and began the Institute for American Church Growth. This institute has had an amazing impact on the congregations and denominations of the United States, Canada, and other "Christian" lands. Every year large numbers of church growth seminars are held all across the country, sometimes on a denominational, sometimes on an inter-denominational basis. The institute has published many books on American church growth. It has made more than a dozen church growth films, many of which are projected each week of the year in congregations all across the United States.

With offices on Colorado Boulevard in Pasadena, the institute has become nationally known. In January of 1987 I spoke at a meeting of more than two hundred denominational executives in Pasadena convened by the Institute for American Church Growth.

Similar influential emphasis on North American church growth was being mounted by Dr. Wagner and his classes on church growth leading to a Doctor of Ministries Degree in Fuller Theological Seminary. Also as the executive secretary for the Fuller Evangelistic Association he held church growth seminars all across the United States. Thus both Dr. Wagner and Dr. Arn have had distinguished ministries in wakening American congregations and denominations to the imperative for church growth and the many opportunities for adding to their own congregations and multiplying new ones. It became increasingly clear that American church growth was a vast field in which many could work effectively.

Indeed, in 1976 the United Methodist Church, observing that it had lost a million members in the previous decade, turned to Dr. George Hunter, gave him a budget of a quarter of a million dollars a year, and asked him to instruct Methodist congregations and conferences all across the land in the principles and practices of church growth. His program did much to turn the United Methodist Church around and, in that denomination, greatly furthered the church growth movement.

After Dr. Arthur Glasser became dean of the School of World Mission on July 1, 1971, the school moved forward rapidly under his direction. More and more attention was paid to Chinese evangelism. More nationals from more countries were given scholarships to the school. The enrollment at the school mounted steadily year by year.

About the same time a business executive, Edward Dayton, who after his conversion decided to become a minister and had enrolled at the Fuller School of Theology, became deeply interested in the School of World Mission and in church growth. He took several courses in the School of World Mission. He contributed the idea of charting the progress of the expansion of Christianity in any given area of people. Upon graduating, he formed a new organization called MARC, Missions Advanced Research and Communications Center. This was made a part of the great World Vision organization. Among its many contributions to the cause is the publication of a series of books titled *Unreached Peoples of the World*.

The Great Commission After the Death of European Imperialism

Essential to an understanding of world mission in the sixties and seventies is a clear picture of the effect that the ending of European imperialism has had on the missionary enterprise. Up until the end of World War II, most of Africa, all of what is now Pakistan, India, Bangladesh, and Burma, all of Indonesia, and the Philippine Islands and sundry other parts of the world were ruled by Western nations. The people of these lands viewed missionaries as a part of Western imperialism. This imperial order collapsed with the end of World War II. The Philippines were granted independence; so was the Indian subcontinent, including Burma. So was Indonesia. During the next fifteen years so were most of the countries in Africa.

With the ending of the imperial era, the national churches in each of these formerly ruled lands, sometimes strong but often weak, insisted more strongly than ever that they were completely independent of Western churches and could neither be ruled by nor guided by missionaries from the West. Mission schools and colleges that had been built, financed, and managed by missionaries speedily appointed national managers and deeded the property to the national churches. Episcopalian churches, most of whose bishops had been Westerners, rapidly retired these and appointed national bishops. The opinions of the national leaders of unions, conferences, dioceses, and synods were increasingly recognized as the last word in what ought to be done. While large amounts of mission money and many missionaries continued to pour into many of these lands, direction of the enterprises was almost entirely in the hands of the national churches concerned.

National governments began to deny visas to missionaries. Whether this governmental action was suggested by leaders of the national churches or by enemies of the Christian faith is not at the present time clear. Both causes have been argued, but the outcome was sharply to diminish the number of missionaries in many nations.

At the very time when many nations of the world were opening to the Christian faith, the number of missionaries who could get permission to work there sharply declined. This led many denominations related to the World Council of Churches to decrease their missionary labors. "World evangelization," they said, "is now the work of the younger churches. We shall continue to make grants to them, but the work is theirs, not ours. Western churches have no desire to continue imperialism."

As a result, the mission budgets of many Western denominations sharply diminished. Since they were no longer sending out large numbers of their own sons and daughters, their giving to missions decreased. For example, the United Presbyterians, who in the fifties were sending out more than sixteen hundred missionaries, in the seventies were sending out fewer than four hundred.

Many evangelical denominations and missionary societies, however, continued to send out missionaries, some even more than before. It was far from settled what world evangelization ought to be in a globe populated by equal nations, most of whom were non-Christians.

Many Christians maintained, "Since in that land we now have our great national church, we no longer need to pray for, give to, and work for that land's evangelization." That this "great church" numbered less than 1 percent of the population of that country did not seem to make much difference to those who advanced this argument.

It was in this kind of a world with these sentiments that the School of World Mission in Pasadena was developing its concepts of what effective missions should be. In the vast enterprise it was easy to do much good work and achieve very little, if any, church growth, i.e., the conversion of large segments of the populations. It was too easy for denominations to "carry on world evangelization" that consisted largely of aiding slow-growing or even nongrowing national churches.

That here and there great growth was occurring did not materially change the picture. For example, while a small denomination known as the Evangelical Church of India was planting one new congregation a week in southern India, and in northeast India the Baptists were adding thousands from the animistic tribes each year, most of the denominations established in the rest of Pakistan, India, Bangladesh, and Burma in the preceding two centuries had become static or slow growing. Some were declining. The rapid growth of the church in Taiwan between 1947 and 1965 had ended. The numbers of Christians there in 1985 remained only slightly larger than they had been in 1965. In Japan only 1 percent of the population had become Christian, and in the Muslim world gate after gate had been shut and locked against any promulgation of the gospel. In the rapidly growing cities of the world also little effective evangelism was being carried out. Segments of the urban populations in many cases were winnable, but they were not being won.

It was this kind of a world that the School of World Mission faced. It was in this kind of a world that the newly named science of missiology made its pronouncements as to how populations ought to be and could be Christianized.

Advances in Church Growth Multiply

The rise of the School of World Mission in Pasadena triggered an increased emphasis on missionary education in evangelical seminaries all across the United States. At Columbia Bible College President Robertson McQuilkin started a graduate department specializing in the preparation and education of missionaries of the church. At Gordon-Conwell Seminary, twenty miles from the great city of Boston, Professor Christy Wilson emphasized Christian mission in a great way. Trinity Divinity School at Deerfield, just north of Chicago, decided to emphasize missions. It sent its new professor of missions, Dr. David Hesselgrave, veteran missionary to Japan, to the Fuller School of World Mission for a full term to learn all that he could and then to launch courses on effective evangelism at Trinity. The Missouri Synod Lutherans appointed a professor of church growth at Concordia Seminary in St. Louis. Biola University, which had had a missions department, strengthened it, appointed four full-time professors of missions and, by the early eighties, had developed a program leading eventually to a Ph.D. in missiology. Westminster Theological Seminary greatly increased its emphasis on effective missions. Dr. Roger Greenway's and Dr. Harvie Conn's courses stressed finding and folding the lost in cities and countrysides. Many other Bible colleges and seminaries introduced courses emphasizing the opportunity and the need to reap fields white to harvest and to care for green fields so that they would shortly become ripe.

Books on mission had been comparatively rare in the fifties and sixties. Such as were published—see the book lists published in the *International Review of Missions* for those years—dealt very seldom with effective evangelism or the discipling of unreached segments of the earth's population. Missions tended to discuss the problems of national churches. The church of Jesus Christ exists in many forms among the many populations of planet earth. Books on missions tended to discuss these problems of existing congregations and denominations, seldom focusing their attention on effective evangelism of non-Christians. To be sure, evangelism was frequently spoken of, but with no distinctions as to whether those who responded to the call were nominal Christians of one's own denomination, nominal Christians of another denomination, the children of Christians, or men and women belonging to some non-Christian faith, such as humanism, Marxism, Buddhism, Islam, or Hinduism.

In sharp contrast, the books published by the Fuller School of World Mission dealt continually with actual Christianization. Was Christ's command to *matheteusate panta ta ethne* really being carried out? To what degree had this *ethnos* or these *ethne* been discipled and enrolled in Christ's body, the church? The career missionaries at the School of World Mission had done careful researches into the multiplication of congregations among various segments of the world's populations. These theses and dissertations were in many cases published. The stream of books relating to effective evangelism formed an ever-widening and deepening stream. Eternal God's command that the gospel be preached to *panta ta ethne* so that these segments of society would be led to faith and obedience was heard, therefore, not merely by professors of mission and students enrolled in missionary courses, but also by the tens of thousands (or more likely hundreds of thousands) who read these books in seminary after seminary and land after land. Dr. Ralph Winter's new publishing house, called the William Carey Library, played a significant part in the publication of these church growth books.

During the seventies the impact of the School of World Mission on the missionary thinking of the Christian world was very considerable among evangelicals. Among conciliars it tended to be ruled out as old fashioned, speaking to a bygone age, unaware of the strong nationalistic sentiments of the younger churches, or not concerned with equality and justice. Nevertheless, bit by bit, here and there, the conciliar denominations were influenced and began to take significant action.

For example, in the early eighties a bishop of the United Methodist Church in the United States, noting that his denomination had lost a million members between 1965 and 1975 and wakened by church growth thinking, proposed that between 1985 and the year 2000 the United Methodist Church win 10 million Americans to ardent Christian faith. What John Wesley had prayed for and dreamed about two hundred years before in England was being envisaged in the United States. Bishop Wilke's dream may not be accomplished, but that it was proposed is vivid illustration of a new burden for church growth. Many denominations were concluding that for them to remain static in the midst of an increasingly humanistic, materialistic, and secular American population was not God's will.

Bible colleges and seminaries also, under the impact of the church growth movement, began to realize that their curricula must include many courses on effective evangelism. American cities were growing increasingly pagan, increasingly secular. Morality in the urban complexes was held to be what 51 percent of the population considered right. A homosexual was elected mayor of San Francisco. Those who regarded the Bible's pronouncements on immorality as the only true morality were held to be "fanatics" or "fundamentalists." Facing this new and increasingly sub-Christian social order, seminary leaders were concluding that much more attention must be paid to the winning of modern urbanites. Biblical congregations must be multiplied in every segment of the vast urban complexes. "We must speak to today," they insisted, "not to yesterday."

As the financial resources available to the School of World Mission increased, other members were added to the faculty and other aspects of the missionary enterprise were taught. For example, since all missionaries need to learn a new language and speak it effectively, a new professor teaching how to learn a new language was added to the faculty.

In an attempt to win a hearing among the widest possible range of denominations, Arthur Glasser and Donald McGavran started teaching a course on contemporary theologies of missions. This dealt with evangelical theology, conciliar theology, Roman Catholic theology, and liberation theology. While describing fairly each of these branches of theology, the course focused on whether a given theology fosters actual obedience to the divine command to win men and women to Christ and multiply Christian congregations. The course later materialized in a book published by Baker Book House called *Contemporary Theologies of Mission*. It became one of the most read books on missions.

Dr. Ralph Winter, the missionary genius who lectured on the history of missions at the School of World Mission, learned that the Pasadena Nazarene College had moved to San Diego and was selling its campus and adjoining lands for $15 million. In 1976 he decided to resign from his post as tenured professor in the School of World Mission to found a world mission center on the former Nazarene campus. The U. S. Center for World Mission became a place where, by 1985, forty missionary organizations, large and small, established their headquarters. Its publications multiplied. It sought to arouse missionary concern in all denominations across America. Dr.Winter insisted that raising the $15 million always be subordinated to raising evangelistic concern in the churches of North America.

The U. S. Center for World Mission further developed the concept of unreached peoples and called sharp attention to the fact that these were not being reached in any adequate way by national churches or by existing missionary efforts. The U. S. Center for World Mission and the several other world mission centers that started in other places, while not calling themselves church growth movements, nevertheless were both a fruit of it and among its most effective promoters.

Time and space will not permit an adequate account of the church growth centers started in other countries of the world, but they must be mentioned. As career missionaries and national leaders graduating from the School of World Mission went back to their lands of labor, they often started church growth centers. These arose in Taiwan, the Philippines, Japan, India, Singapore, Kenya, Brazil, England, Germany, and Australia. The attention of missionary societies and churches was increasingly focused on carrying out eternal God's command and obeying Him to whom all authority in heaven and earth had been given.

In 1980 Arthur Glasser resigned as dean and continued teaching. His place was taken by Dr. Paul Pierson, a United Presbyterian missionary to Brazil for many years. Under his dynamic leadership the school increased still more. The extension services begun in the early seventies and directed by Dr. Alvin Martin influenced hundreds overseas. Nationals and missionaries, while residing in other lands, took accredited courses from the School of World Mission.

When the School of World Mission opened on September 25, 1985, 277 students from seventy-two different nations, including—wonder of wonders—Yugoslavia and Namibia, registered on campus. Twenty-two Ph.D. degrees in missiology had been given, 151 professional doctorates in missiology, and very large numbers of M.Th. and M.A. degrees in missiology had been conferred upon men and women who had successfully completed strenuous courses on missiology. Most of these have been career missionaries and national leaders, though some were missionary candidates.

This chapter, covering the years 1971–85, indicates some of the impact of the ever-widening church growth thinking.

10

Ideological and Theological Concerns

The church growth movement thrives in a very complex world. Indeed, it advocates effective evangelism in a world where many others are advocating other useful and necessary courses of action. This has often produced vigorous attacks on the idea of church growth. This chapter will devote attention to three of the main areas of clash.

Social Justice and Church Growth

Social justice is urgently needed. Today's world has shrunk into a very small place. In fewer hours than it used to take to travel from New York to Philadelphia it is now possible to travel from New York to Singapore, Zambia, or Argentina. One world has come into being. The concept of many equal nations is rapidly pushing out the concept of civilized and backward peoples. If the population of east Africa is suffering from an enormous famine, it ought not to be so. If four thousand are killed in Mexico City by a great earthquake, many nations rush doctors and aid of many sorts to Mexico City. This is certainly not the world in which David Livingstone and William Carey lived. Hundreds of thousands of students from Asia and Africa flood into Europe and America. Large numbers of European and American students travel in other countries as part of their education. The tidal wave of secularism that has swept Western countries declares that all religions have some truth in them. Therefore, world evangelization by Christians is an outmoded idea.

As Christians look out on this kind of a world, they too are powerfully moved toward rectifying the physical and social conditions that produce famine, illiteracy, and disease. They too feel a great urge to wipe out injustice and oppression. Although the media speak very little about the tremendous oppressions carried out by Marxist governments scattered throughout the world, they focus enormous attention on South Africa. Government after government brings pressure on the South African government to change its ways. Enthusiasts for social justice exclaim, "Of what use is it to make men and women Christian if they are being treated unfairly by the powerful in their populations?" Here in North America also the need for Christians to take vigorous action against the oppressions suffered by blacks and minorities claims a great deal of attention.

What does the church growth movement say to this passion for justice and brotherhood? It says three things. First, it rejoices that justice is beginning to roll down like the waters and that a mighty stream of righteousness is beginning to be felt in many parts of the world.

Second, the church growth movement maintains that this concern that all segments of society, the one hundred thousand or more people groups, be treated fairly is basically a Christian concern. When the population of the world has become more Christian, it will hear almighty God's command to treat other men fairly and to obey that command more faithfully. It is useless to expect that non-Christians will be as interested as Christians in treating all men as God's children. If we want mercy, justice, and righteousness to spread throughout the earth, we can take no more effective action than to multiply congregations of the redeemed in every segment of society. No one will act more justly toward his or her fellows than those who live in Christ and whose lives are guided by the Holy Spirit.

Third, the church growth movement insists that while the church ought certainly to carry out other activities, such as worship, the instruction of Christian children, the feeding of the poor, and the promotion of justice, for example, it must devote a larger share of its resources, its prayers, and its power to proclaiming the gospel, finding the lost, and bringing them home to the Father's house. Only so will the kingdom of God really come on earth.

The kingdom of God is one in which the King—Lord Jesus—is

recognized. Where the King is not recognized, the kingdom of God is yet to come.

Structural Unity and Church Growth

The second concept that has attracted enormous attention among many denominations is that of the *structural* unity of the universal church. The Lord Jesus certainly said, "I will build my church, and the gates of hell will not prevail against it." He did not say "churches." The church of Jesus Christ is, therefore, one.

On this biblical basis many have inferred that the church is *structurally* one. It has one name, one set of bishops or administrators, one organization, one leader, and one theology. The Roman Catholic Church holds this position very vigorously. The idea of the structural unity of the church has become a very powerful influence among many denominations today; my own, the Disciples of Christ, is a notable example.

One thinks immediately of COCU, Churches of Christ Uniting. When it was first launched, it held the appealing idea that the union of six or seven of America's largest denominations was both God's will and feasible. One great church with 35 million members or more would dominate North America. Structural unity is held to be more economical. The resulting church is held to be more powerful. It will, it is argued, be able to do God's will much more effectively than a church consisting of many denominations. This concept of one structurally united church has become the main drive in the lives of many Christians and many congregations. Whether they win others to Christ or not, they are going to unite. Two weak churches are going to become one strong church. The United Church of Christ, the United Methodist Church, and the Presbyterian Church in the U.S.A. are three notable illustrations of this movement.

In India, where this movement has been greatly promoted by the Episcopalian Church, two great united churches have resulted—the Church of North India and the Church of South India. Their adherents number less than two million of the eight million Protestants. Both of these believe in apostolic succession, i.e., the historical episcopate, and both are ardent Episcopal churches.

What do we say to this second great movement of today's denominations?

First, we grant that in many circumstances structural unity does produce a more efficient organization. We also note that in many cases the structurally united church is much less concerned with world evangelization than it was in the days before the several denominations united. We call attention to the diminishing effectiveness of united churches in all outreach. They are so concerned with maintaining internal unity that their outreach efforts are sadly diminished.

No evidence indicates that a universal church structurally united is more effective evangelistically than a universal church consisting of many branches or denominations structurally separate but united in regard to beliefs in Christ and the Bible. Each denomination is a separate branch of the one universal church. This branch has fifteen leaves on it, that one has fifteen hundred. This one bears white grapes, that one bears purple grapes. As long as each branch is firmly in the vine, as long as each branch believes on Jesus Christ as God and only Savior and the Bible as the inspired and totally reliable Word of God, real differences in regard to baptism, ecclesiastical organization, and other less central doctrines can be tolerated.

Each denomination will certainly follow its own convictions, but it will not affirm that those following other understandings of the Scripture are no part of the true church. Lutherans will certainly interpret the Scripture in ways different from Baptists or Presbyterians. Pentecostals will emphasize aspects of the Scripture ignored by Congregationalists. But as long as a denomination believes in Jesus as God and Savior and the Bible as God's Word, it is a branch of the true church. One denomination will certainly regret what it sees as misunderstandings of Scripture held by another branch, but it will not hold that the other denomination is no part of the true church. This branch, like the Anglican Church, may believe in apostolic succession. That branch, like the Southern Baptists, may not. The body of Christ, the church, has many parts as dissimilar as hands and head. Yet they are all parts of the body.

Where structural unity advances the discipling of the peoples of

the earth, by all means promote it. But never substitute it for effective evangelism, the work so clearly commanded by God. Structural
unity is like many other good causes. They should be carried out, *but
none of them should ever be substituted for the direct command of the
ultimate Authority in the universe, matheteusate panta ta ethne.* None
should be substituted for finding lost sons and daughters and
bringing them back to the Father's house.

Theological Convictions and Church Growth

The third important concept dealt with in this chapter is the
theological considerations that affect the church growth movement.
The church growth movement has often been criticized on theological grounds, from both the right and the left. Those on the right have
maintained that it pays too little attention to correct doctrine, infilling of the Holy Spirit, prayer, revival, and the active Christian life.
Critics from the left have maintained that the church growth movement seems unaware of the physical hunger in the world, the rank
injustice that permeates all society, the terrible oppressions that
have kept whole races in an illiterate and scarcely human condition.
Critics of the left have maintained that church growth theology—
what there is of it—is concerned with mere numbers.

The church growth movement, however, believes itself to be
basically sound in theology. It is advocating church growth on
unassailable biblical grounds. It assumes that church growth will be
carried out chiefly by those who are born-again Christians filled
with the Holy Spirit. How, then, to respond to this criticism from
the right and from the left? What does the church growth movement
answer to its critics?

First, it points out that the church growth movement has arisen on
interdenominational grounds. Its founder wrote his first book, *The
Bridges of God*, not for his own denomination or missionary society
but for all denominations and all missionary societies. *The Bridges of
God* dealt with Christian mission as it was being carried on in all
countries by all advocates of the gospel. Furthermore, as the movement incorporated itself, first in the Institute of Church Growth and
then in the School of World Mission, these were essentially inter-

denominational institutions. At the School of World Mission career missionaries and other students have come from more than seventy denominations. The faculty at both the Institute of Church Growth and the School of World Mission was composed of men from many branches of the church. Yet they were all basically united in one concern, that God's command to effectively evangelize the peoples of the world be carried out.

How did this interdenominational setting affect the theology of the church growth movement? The first answer to this question is that the data regarding effective evangelism was drawn from many different actual situations, many different national churches fathered by denominations as distinct as the Pentecostal and the Presbyterian, the Christian Reformed of Grand Rapids, Michigan, and the United Church of Christ. Even some Roman Catholics have studied at the School of World Mission. One man, Dr. Donald Wodarz, of the Gregorian University in Rome, spent a year at the School of World Mission writing his dissertation on church growth missiology.

All this had an inevitable theological result. *Distinctive* doctrines of different denominations were seldom mentioned. The form of baptism—whether by immersion of believers or the sprinkling of infants—was never discussed. God was blessing advocates of both positions. Some faculty members of the School of World Mission held one view and some another. To debate the mode of baptism would not advance the cause of effective evangelism. Many other similar illustrations could be given.

The common beliefs were what *were* stressed, the common theological foundation stones. The theology emphasized by the church growth movement arising from the School of World Mission and Institute of Church Growth has inevitably been criticized by people of both right and left, who have not found in it certain distinctive doctrines they hold dear.

The second cause for the criticism of the theology of the church growth movement stemmed from the reluctance of those who were not getting church growth—whether in the United States or the Republic of Zaire or some other country—to be measured by their achievements in church growth. They were doing many other good things. They were stressing many good doctrines. They were living good lives. They were engaged in prayer. What matter if in the past decade they had won very few non-Christians to the Christian faith?

The church growth movement acknowledges that even the most ardent evangelists, most concerned to carry out the Great Commission, do often find themselves in resistant populations where, no matter how well the gospel is proclaimed, few are baptized. Nevertheless, the church growth movement maintains that the central purpose of all evangelism must be finding the lost and bringing them back to the fold. The shepherd must not go out simply to tour the hillsides and ravines shouting the good news that there is a sheepfold. He must find the lost and *bring them back to the fold*. When sent into a ripe field, he must intend to bring out a sheaf every two minutes. He must realize that the Lord Jesus came to seek and save the lost, and he must do the same.

A theological concern of the greatest importance must now be mentioned. It can be summed up in a proposition. Each denomination (each branch of the true church) ought to construct a theology that *demands* church growth in keeping with its particular theological emphasis. As, for example, Pentecostals emphasize speaking in tongues (which most writers on church growth have not discussed), they must not do so to the neglect of church growth. Among various theological groups, whether Presbyterians, Lutherans, Baptists, or Methodists, church growth must be an integral part of their theology, and not a detached principle or afterthought.

It is no accident that Dr. George Hunter, dean of the E. Stanley Jones School of World Mission and Evangelism at Asbury Seminary, on reading carefully John Wesley's writings, discovered that Wesley used what are now called church growth principles. In short, every denomination can—and must—present its church growth programs in the light of its own firmly held theology.

These chapters have laid great emphasis upon the New Testament mandate for effective discipling. Those engaging in church growth are not pursuing the latest fad. They are emphasizing essential Christianity. As we talk about the multitudes of static, nongrowing congregations here in North America, we are talking about assemblages of Christians who desperately need to hear and obey eternal God's command. We are talking to Christians standing in the midst of spiritually starving thousands. The Christians have their hands on bags of bread, securely tied. Today's Christians need to open their bags and distribute the bread. We are talking about church members and pastors who need to realize that any truly Christian congregation will devote a considerable portion of its prayers, finances, conversation, sermons, and worship to discipling numbers of the unreached at home and abroad. These are dying in the midst of a terrible famine brought on by secularism, agnosticism, humanism, and non-Christian religions.

Any truly Christian theology in the most responsive world ever to exist must demand church growth. Any fully Christian theology in America, where at least four-fifths of the population is either very nominally Christian or totally non-Christian, must pray for, give to, and work for substantial church growth.

11

Segments of Society and Church Growth

Humanity is a vast mosaic of tens of thousands of pieces. When someone goes to Mexico City and walks past the wall of the university library, he sees a mosaic covering that wall. He sees a one-hundred-yard-long picture composed not of paint but of millions of pieces of colored glass—some blue, some red, some purple, some gray, some white, some black. That mosaic typifies humanity.

Is this view of humankind biblically sound? Of course it is! The Old Testament is full of peoples, tribes, and separate segments of humanity—the Moabites, Ammonites, Hivites, Perizzites, Philistines, Syrians, Egyptians, and on and on. Even in Israel there were twelve tribes, each of which considered itself quite separate from the others.

In our Lord's day the Levites were very careful to marry Levites. Only such Levites as had an impeccable Levitical ancestry on both sides of the family could serve as priests in the temple.

When we come to the New Testament, we find that the command to proclaim the gospel to all *peoples* emphasizes this segmental characteristic. The command is *matheteusate panta ta ethne*. We are not told to *matheteusate* all the millions of men and women. We are told to *matheteusate panta ta ethne*, all the ethnic units, all the groups of people, all the segments of society, all the pieces of the vast human mosaic.

Today we are very likely to think in terms of evangelizing nation-states—the United States, China, Japan, Zaire, Argentina, Venezuela, and so on. Never once in the New Testament is there a command to evangelize the Roman Empire. The command is to evangelize *panta ta ethne*. The New Testament is very clear that the segments of society, the pieces of the mosaic, are to be evangelized, discipled, and made parts of the body of Christ.

In Revelation we read that at the end men and women will be there from every tribe and tongue and people and nation (Rev. 5:9). The Bible clearly intends that we evangelize all pieces of the mosaic— all *ethne*.

It is necessary today to emphasize this because in America, this vast nation which spreads from the Atlantic to the Pacific, we are constantly emphasizing that we are one people. We must not allow the Cubans flooding into Florida or the Mexicans flooding into California to continue to speak Spanish alone. English must become the one national language. Women and men of every part of the mosaic must receive the same wages for the same work. Equal education must be available to all of them. They are all Americans. Facing this overwhelming conviction, Christian radio has come to the conclusion that the gospel must be broadcast to all, and those whom God chooses from every segment of society will join "our church." When one becomes a Christian, a Spirit-filled follower of the Lord Jesus, a Bible-obeying person, he or she is then part of a new order of society in which there is no Jew, no Greek, no slave, no free, no male, no female.

However, despite both the secular nationalistic thrust for unity and the Christian conviction that maintains that all Christians are equally saved, the various branches of the church have gathered unto themselves like-minded people. For example, Ray Bakke has a pertinent paragraph in *An Urban World: Churches Facing the Future,* in which he says: "Chicago—formerly an ethnic European city—is rapidly Asianizing. Houston public schools are now 80% Black, Hispanic, and Asian. . . . 'Boat people' from South East Asia, hitherto unaccessible to the gospel, are finding Christ in Chicago."[1]

Urban humanity is a mosaic made up of thousands of pieces. Men and women of each piece like to join congregations made up of people like themselves, speaking the same language, receiving the same incomes, having the same amount of education, and thinking very much alike.

The latter half of the twentieth century is seeing tremendous

1. Nashville: Broadman Press, 1984, pp. 78-79.

urbanization. It is estimated that by the year 2000 more than half of the population of the world will live in great cities. Mexico City is only one example. Calcutta, Delhi, Bombay, and many other cities in India together with Hong Kong, Singapore, Manila, Tokyo, Seoul, and an ever greater number in Europe and the Americas furnish other examples.

As Professor James Westgate has so well said:

> The birth and growth of world class cities is a new frontier for the evangelist and church planter. The world's population has migrated to the cities and this migration has given birth to cities larger than ever existed. They are called world class cities because they are tied technologically and economically to other major urban centers around the world. . . . demographers [say] that by the year 2000, we will see the emergence of sixty cities over five million people, twenty-five cities over ten million people, and five cities over twenty million people.[2]

Dr. Roger Greenway, in his magazine *Urban Mission*, has done a great service to Christ's cause in emphasizing effective evangelization of this great urban population, which by the year 2000 will include more than half of all the people in the world.

As the Great Commission is carried out, as all the ethnic units, all segments of society, are discipled, the church of Jesus Christ will continue to be made up of a vast number of Christianized segments. Because they are Christianized, they will grow increasingly like each other in certain respects. However, the differences of language, culture, income, and place of residence will continue. *Congregations ought to be multiplied in each piece of the mosaic.*

The modern city is not made up of one kind of persons but of many, many different kinds—business executives, government officers, daily laborers, university professors, ditch diggers, illiterates, semiliterates, and many, many others. In some segments of America the average income is $50,000 a year; in others it is $5,000.

Stated in ethnic terms, urban populations in America today are composed of many different ethnic strains—Anglos, blacks, Hispanics, Vietnamese, Chinese, Filipinos, Samoans, French Ca-

2. James Westgate, "Emerging Church Planting Strategies for World Class Cities," *Trinity World Forum*, 10, 3 (Summer 1985): 3-4.

nadians, and many others. Each of these major di
divided into subsections. Recent arrivals from Mexico
from third and fourth generation Hispanics. Puerto Rican Hispanic
consider themselves superior to Mexican Hispanics. And Argen-
tinian Hispanics hold themselves to be superior to Puerto Ricans.
The mosaic of humanity is wonderfully displayed in American cities
today.

Each segment must be won to Christ on its own level. If it is
invited to join a church composed of people living on a different
level, it will reject Christ very largely because the Savior is obscured
by His congregation. Let me give you some examples to drive home
this essential truth.

In the mid-sixties I was conducting a church growth seminar in
the Tenth Presbyterian Church of Philadelphia. After one of the
sessions I fell into conversation with Dr. C. Everett Koop, who later
became surgeon general of the United States. He said to me, "A
black tide has swept up around this old church on three sides. Large
numbers of men and women from the deep south now live as our
close neighbors. They do not, however, attend our church. What
ought we to do to win them to Christ?"

I replied, "You must become an integrated church."

"We are an integrated church," he responded. "We have at least
fifteen black families as members of our congregation."

"What then is your problem?" I asked in amazement.

"Our black families drive in from the suburbs. They include none
of the blacks living in the immediate neighborhood."

Immediately a picture of the exact situation formed in my mind.
The blacks living in the suburbs were affluent blacks, college graduates who held good positions. The blacks from the deep south who
lived around the church were of a very different culture, income,
and education. Had they attended the Tenth Presbyterian Church,
they would not have fully understood the sermons or the hymns.

"If the Tenth Presbyterian Church is to win your close neighbors
to Christian faith," I replied, "it must start many house churches
among them, within—let us say—a mile or two of the church buildings. These new congregations would be led by black ministers of
eighth-grade education or less."

"Dr. McGavran!" exclaimed Dr. Koop. "Presbyterians never have any ministers of eighth-grade education or less!"

The second illustration of the fragmented nature of American society presents one of the many segments of white society. Americans are divided not merely into whites and blacks but into many kinds of whites and many kinds of blacks. In addition, there are many kinds of Chinese, Portuguese, French Canadians, secularists, and humanists. Some of these can, of course, be successfully incorporated into existing congregations or discipled into new congregations. In the congregation in Philippi, we remember, there were both Lydia, a cloth merchant, and an unnamed jailer, who was socially and economically a long distance removed from her.

Nevertheless, until Christians see these distinctions and plan to multiply Christian congregations (house churches or cells) in each unreached segment of society, we shall not see the kind of church growth that God desires and is now quite possible.

I must mention here the experience of the South Gate Presbyterian Church in Denver, Colorado. In 1975 it noted that its membership had decreased from over twelve hundred to under seven hundred and was sinking every year. Its pastor decided to call Dr. Win Arn, the founder of the Institute for American Church Growth, and me to hold a church growth seminar, at which 85 percent of the attendants were members of his church. As Dr. Arn and I prepared for this seminar, we made a careful study of what had actually happened. The picture was quite clear. Nearly half of the members of that congregation had moved from a section of the city around the church out to the more attractive suburbs of Denver. Another group of Anglos had moved in but had not joined the church. Surrounding the church was a different segment of the Anglo population. It could have been won, had the South Gate Presbyterians been passionately concerned with church growth. Had they been Pentecostals filled with the Holy Spirit, they would have prayed for these people, started new groups of the redeemed among them, and wooed them into the church. Here effective evangelism could have won them. But that evangelism would have been considerably warmer and more effective than those Presbyterians were employing.

Consequently, Dr. Arn and I spoke of two needs. First, the South

Gate Presbyterian Church should make a definite effort to win to Christ scores of men and women in their neighborhood. Second, those won should be organized into Sunday school classes, prayer groups, and church committees where the newcomers formed a majority. If this were done, the South Gate Presbyterian Church would be seen by the newcomers as "a church where we feel at home."

The mosaic of humanity is a social actuality, which all those who obey eternal God's command must take into account. It must not be supposed that society is made up of one kind of people. Every segment of humankind and especially of urban humanity must find *multiplying within it* congregations of the redeemed. As this occurs, these will bring about a new sense of brotherhood, equality, and human oneness.

This new humanity, however, will not be secular, humanistic, and immoral. It will not believe that all people, no matter what their religion or lack of religion may be, are essentially one. That humanist view, which is sweeping the Western world at the present time, is taking increasingly large numbers in America into an immoral social order. Committed Christians, however, insist that while the different segments of humanity must be treated with love, justice, kindness, and righteousness, the Christian movement enrolls only such as determine to live in Christ. The tens of thousands of house churches, Sunday school classes, evangelistic Bible studies, and the like will do two things. They will win unbelievers to Christ and will work to bring about the rule of brotherhood, love, and justice in all pieces of the mosaic.

Brotherhood will not destroy the pieces of the mosaic. They will continue on. We read in Revelation 7:9 that at the end before the throne and the Lamb there will be "a great multitude . . . from every *ethne,* tribe, people, and language." All these will be Christians. All these will love all other Christians. All these will promote brotherhood and justice and kindness and righteousness. But they will not wipe out the social, linguistic, and economic distinctions. The segments of humanity will continue until the end. The vast human mosaic will still be there. But its sinful aspects will have been eliminated. That is clear.

Church growth ardently maintains that we must continue to recognize that humanity is a mosaic. Into every piece must flow the redeeming power of Jesus Christ. The growth of the church will not meld green, white, black, yellow, purple, and red pieces of the mosaic into one dark grey piece. No, the red will remain red, the white will remain white, the purple will remain purple. But in each of the thousands of ethnic units societies of the redeemed will multiply.

Not only will societies of the redeemed multiply but they will also break down and wash away the hates, oppressions, prides, and persecutions that in the unredeemed world always mar the mosaic. It will remain, but it will be a redeemed mosaic.

As schools of theological education come to realize this aspect of humanity and multiply courses in effective evangelism, God will use them much more potently for discipling all the *ethne* in the world.

Dr. Greenway has stated this emphatically:

> . . . we must hold tenaciously to the goal of vital Christian churches established and growing in each and every people group in the city, glorifying God in their own language and culture form, advancing Christ's kingdom to the outer limits of their community" (*Urban Mission* [May, 1985], p. 5).

12

Seeing the Actual Facts

Are We Working Blindfolded in Our Churches?

In many congregations, denominations, Bible schools, and seminaries good Christians—lay and clerics—are engaged in many good works and do not really see the church growth situation. They are not vividly conscious of where their new members are coming from. They do not know which segments of society are responsive. Theological schools are resigned to whatever degree of growth or decline the ministers they train are securing. They do not believe that every church should be giving birth to new congregations. In short, they go into the white fields blindfolded. They are theologically sound in regard to many doctrines, but in regard to eternal God's command to proclaim the gospel to all segments of society throughout the entire world, leading people to faith and obedience, they are quite unsound. They know a great deal about the Bible, live good moral lives, but neither see the ripe fields nor bring in many sheaves.

The minister of a large congregation in Vancouver, Washington, some years ago told me contentedly, "We win some fifty or sixty new members every year. That keeps this church quite healthy and vigorous." I asked him how many of these new members are the result of biological growth, transfer growth, or conversion growth. He replied, "I don't know what you mean." I explained. He replied, "That is very interesting. I don't know, but I'll find out."

A day later he called me saying, "Sixteen of the fifty members we added last year were children of our members—biological growth. Thirty were Christians who had moved to Vancouver from other cities—transfer growth. Only four, I fear, were converts from the world—conversion growth." He added, "I am amazed at the small number of converts."

His own city church might be growing a little, but his denomination in that part of the world was standing still. It was not winning many of the 70 percent of the population that had little or no church allegiance.

I carefully studied two great mission stations in the heart of Africa. In the previous seventeen years the Christians in station Dombe had increased from three thousand to thirty-three thousand. In station Yeka the Christians had decreased from seven thousand to three thousand. Each of these stations was manned by eight missionaries and cost the home board about the same number of dollars.

When I stated this finding to the home board in the United States, I was assured that I must be wrong. Such a thing could not be. The executive for Africa said emphatically, "While I do not know the actual facts, I am sure that your report is wrong." But when further investigation proved that my report was correct, he realized that the mission board had been carrying on missions blindfolded. While they spent much money doing many good works—evangelism, education, medicine, and leprosy work—they had not spent a single dime in assembling the facts as to what growth was taking place, where it was coming from, and what needed to be done to assure even greater growth in the future. Hundreds of similar illustrations could be given.

In the early seventies the School of World Mission in Pasadena held a seminar for pastors of Hispanic congregations of many denominations. For three days they studied church growth. On the third day I was talking to a pastor of a Hispanic congregation of some three hundred members. I asked him who were the most responsive of the 25 million Hispanics now in the United States.

He replied quickly, "Oh, the recent arrivals."

I asked him, "If you were to seek to win these into your congregation, could you succeed?"

Without a moment's hesitation he replied, "Man, they would swamp us!"

His congregation was made up of respectable, well-to-do, second-, third- and fourth-generation Hispanics and did not want a lot of recent immigrants. They would bring in too many problems. Furthermore, they would not understand his carefully prepared sermons. They wouldn't know that much English. Nor would they speak his type of Spanish.

If we are to carry out Christ's command to disciple all the peoples of the world, we must take off the blindfolds. Seminaries and denominations must do whatever research is necessary to find out the actual facts. We must discover which ways of proclaiming the gospel God is blessing to the increase of His church and which ways He is not. Believe me, many ways of carrying on the work of the church are sound in regard to many aspects of theology and academically quite impressive. Yet they try to bring back very few lost sheep. At that point they are theologically quite unsound.

Schools of theological education must know and teach which are the ripe fields and what methods of reaping in each are being blessed by God. Church growth research on a thoroughly reliable basis must have a high priority in every Bible college and seminary program. Only as pastors and ministers in training see exactly which of the many congregations of their denominations are growing and which are not, how much they are growing, and from what segments of society they are growing will pastors be able both to maintain their present congregations and to be evangelistically effective. Only so will they save America from becoming an ever more secular and pagan society.

Double Your Denomination in Ten Years

Goal setting is important. So is research that tells us how far the goals are being achieved.

In 1976 an ardent denomination, the Christian and Missionary Alliance, decided prayerfully to set a goal of doubling its membership in the next ten years, so that by 1987 both in North America and around the world it would have twice as many members. In 1984 I wrote to the chief executive of that denomination in Nyack, New York. He replied that the denomination's worldwide membership would more than double but that in North America they might lag a little behind their goal. The Alliance not only set that goal but insisted that in all the countries where Alliance churches were found careful records as to growth should be kept. Every minister and every missionary, therefore, found out how fast his church was growing, from what segments of society it was growing, and what ways of evangelism God was blessing.

Goal setting and careful research as to the degree of growth achieved are something that every seminary, denomination, and congregation can easily inaugurate. As Bible colleges and seminaries train future pastors, preachers, and missionaries, they must give them an accurate picture as to how the *ethne* in their parts of the world are being discipled. They must teach what parts of the task have been completed and what parts yet need to begin. A correct theology will be most effective only as it is united with an accurate picture of what correct theology means in the mosaic that surrounds us. Every theological school ought to have a full-time professor constantly drawing and redrawing accurate pictures of the degree to which *panta ta ethne* are being added to the body of Christ in congregations pastored by their graduates. At present the typical denomination executive, minister, or—I am sorry to say—theological professor is not keenly aware of the growth or decline patterns that mark his congregations and denomination. It remains true that among the most orthodox and biblical denominations in America are also found some of the least growing. This woeful situation ought to be and can be corrected.

One of my students did a very careful survey of the Conservative Baptist denomination. He found that during the forties and early fifties it grew rapidly. But after that it slowed down and was in danger of becoming static. He also found that this early rapid growth came as congregations of the Northern Baptist Church, displeased with the liberalism of many of their leaders and seminaries, decided to join the Conservative Baptist denomination. Growth was taking place not from the world but from existing Christians. When all those who wished to leave the Northern Baptists had done so, growth almost stopped.

This research also revealed that while the Conservative Baptists as a whole had slowed down, here and there individual congregations were growing rapidly. A few were planting new congregations. Evidently growth was to be had if pastors wanted it. Those congregations whose ministers and laymen were obeying Christ's commands were growing. Those who were not obeying were not growing. They were, to be sure, doing many good works, preaching biblical sermons, and conducting impressive worship. But they were not finding many of the lost.

This research, while factually correct, was not welcomed by the leaders of the Conservative Baptist denomination. It did, however, play a considerable part in arousing them to the situation. The Conservative Baptists, like all other denominations, can grow in the United States today, provided they determine to. If they will but pray the Lord of the harvest to send forth laborers into the harvest and see the actual facts about church growth, God will bless them with much church growth. If they will make five courses in effective evangelism required in all their theological training schools, they will experience a tremendous burst of growth.

Multiplying New Congregations Is Important

Dr. George Hunter III, dean of the E. Stanley Jones School of World Mission and Evangelism in Asbury Theological Seminary, is a specialist in effective evangelism. His significant book *To Spread the Power* is available from Abingdon Press. The book is full of important information about how congregations and denominations today can be theologically sound in regard to carrying out God's repeated commands to spread the gospel and the power. Illustrations are given from the United States and other lands.

In chapter 5 we find the following figures about the growth of six denominations in the Philippines in 1971–81. The Christian and Missionary Alliance grew from 22,000 members to 70,000. That is significant decadal growth indeed. The Wesleyan Church grew from 2,400 members to 7,000 members, the Nazarenes from 937 to 6,000, the Convention Baptists from 34,000 to 56,000, the Southern Baptists from 15,000 to 61,000, and the Conservative Baptists from 1,600 to 10,000.

Turning to the United States, Dr. Hunter says, "In the U.S.A. today, in most years, the denominations that are growing are starting more churches than they are closing" ([1987], 111). The entire volume is well worth reading. It casts much light on how congregations and denominations can grow. Most importantly it arouses theological schools to the essential task of preparing ministers who know the essential facts and are therefore effective in finding God's lost sons and daughters and bringing them home.

Exact Knowledge About New Ethne

If branches of the universal church are to obey eternal God's command, they must frequently give birth to new congregations in new segments of the population. In addition they must know where and to what degree they are doing this. This principle is usually not seen. Yet it has an easily observable relationship to reaping ripe fields. Those congregations and denominations grow which discover unharvested ripe fields and multiply new congregations among them. Those congregations and denominations which do not grow as a rule are confining themselves to their own partially discipled segment of the population.

Courses dealing with this aspect of the task in the modern world must be taught in every school of theological education. An exact picture of the true situation in each denomination concerned and of how the situation can be improved must be taught. Exact facts must be compiled for the many pieces of the American mosaic. The situation varies from state to state and, indeed, county to county. A true picture of the hundreds of different opportunities and difficulties in this complicated growth pattern is a necessary part of the education of future pastors.

A splendid illustration of this point is the city-wide research done in Philadelphia by Westminster Theological Seminary under the direction of Professors Roger Greenway and Harvie Conn. It was discovered that in Philadelphia there live fifty-one different minority groups and that most of these are woefully underchurched. The women and men in these groups are eagerly trying to become better Americans. The resulting opportunities for proclaiming the gospel and multiplying churches in each minority are great.

Westminster Theological Seminary has a branch in an elegant old house near the heart of the city. Here students—some of them are pastors—come from various minorities. New congregations are being started by these students in their communities. Consequently, Westminster Seminary is vividly aware of the opportunities offered by the various pieces of the Philadelphia mosaic. If every seminary and Bible college in the United States and Canada were to conduct similar researches into the actual evangelistic opportunities in its own urban community and were to teach this true and accurate picture of the contemporary situation, the command of the ultimate Authority in the universe (Matt. 28:18) would be much more effectively carried out.

For example, in 1983 it was my privilege to speak to the Church Extension Department of the Southern Baptists in Texas. The executive secretary of this state organization said, "In Texas we have 4,000 Baptist churches. We have determined to plant 2,000 more by the year 1990. This means that we will be planting about 300 new congregations a year. Of these new churches, 45 percent will be among Anglos, 40 percent among Hispanics, and 15 percent among other ethnic groups."

Later I was talking to the pastor of a large Baptist church in east Houston. He said, "Near where I work is a section of the city in which there live fifteen thousand people. We are starting four new Baptist congregations there."

I remarked, "I am surprised that in Houston there is any section of the city with a population of fifteen thousand in which there are not already several Baptist churches."

"Oh," he replied,"we do have two Baptist churches there, but they are more than fifty years old, and their members are well-to-do middle class people. Most of the other people in this section of the city are working-class Anglos. Since they do not as a rule join middle-class churches, we are planning to start four congregations of working-class people. We already have seven house gatherings of two or three families and four house churches of six or eight families. Within a year or two we will have at least two new Baptist congregations thriving in that part of the city, and by 1990 we will have at least four."

Both the Church Extension Department and this one pastor in east Houston were acting with exact knowledge of the multitudinous segments of society that compose the population of Texas.

As already stated, Kittel defines an *ethnos* as a group of similar individuals—a swarm of bees or a herd of cattle is an *ethnos*. In a similar fashion middle-class Anglos are one *ethnos*, and blue-collar Anglos are another *ethnos*. Each must be discipled, that is, incorporated into the body of Christ. In short, congregations of baptized believers must be multiplied in each *ethnos*. Only so can any *ethnos* be discipled. If we are to carry out the clear command of Him to whom all authority in heaven and earth has been given, we must disciple *ethnos* after *ethnos*, both in the United States and around the world.

In the United States the multitudinous *ethne* (segments of the population) are not highly visible. We are all American citizens. We all speak English. We all are free. There is no apartheid here. Yet as we have seen again and again many such segments of the population do exist in the United States. *And we need exact information about how each is being discipled.*

In many countries of the world, notably India and Africa, caste and tribe divisions are very much more clearly marked. Men belonging to the Narmadiya Brahmins will never intermarry with Kankubj Brahmins. Both, to be sure, are Brahmins. But each is keenly conscious of its existence as a separate unit of society. It intends to remain separate. There are at least three thousand such castes in India.

Each African nation is full of not Africans but tribes. In the great country of Zaire there are 127 tribes. Each not only intermarries very largely within itself but speaks a different language or dialect and thinks of itself as an entirely separate people, just as separate as the Amorites, Perizzites, and Israelites were fifteen hundred years before Christ.

It is essential, therefore, not only in the United States but around the world to realize that carrying out eternal God's command can be done only by exact knowledge as to these different segments, their responsiveness or resistance to the gospel, and other factors related to their discipling. Exact knowledge is essential.

How Many of the 340,000 Congregations in the United States Are Growing?

The number of congregations that are growing, static, or declining is not known. Furthermore, why each is growing, static, or declining is not known.

This information is readily available. It can be discovered. It can be exactly stated. But this is seldom done. Many excellent congregations, pastored by devoted ministers, remain static or declining. This is so common that most ministers and seminary professors tend to view the whole duty of the minister as preaching theologically sound and well-expressed sermons, caring for and loving the flock, and leading an exemplary life. If he does this and God wills, his congregation will grow. He should not be concerned with increasing mere numbers.

Let me emphasize again that no one is advocating multiplying unconverted, nominal Christians. No one is advocating adding "mere numbers." Effective evangelism never brings in merely an additional warm body. Church growth is as much concerned with soundly Christian life as with finding the lost. Be assured that the lost are never truly found until they are incorporated in the flock, obey the Shepherd, walk in His way, and are filled with the Holy Spirit.

We now come to a most important question. Every school of theological education serves a specific denomination or cluster of denominations. It is supported by donors from these. Each faculty should ask: What effect does study here have on the growth of the congregations and denominations our graduates will serve and from which our faculty have come? What are the growth patterns that mark the congregations to which our graduates will go? To be specific, let professors in each seminary and Bible college ask, How are our congregations at finding the lost and reaping white harvest fields? Have we secured exact knowledge concerning each of the many different kinds of white harvest fields that surround this theological school?

Such questions bring sharply to the fore the need for accurate information. In each of the many clusters of congregations there may be fifteen or more congregations. Each one of them faces different opportunities for effective evangelism. Each one has a different awareness of how greatly God desires—indeed commands—that particular *ethnos* to be discipled. This one will regard church growth as of no importance. That one is working hard at it. This pastor hopes that his sermons and his services will bring many to his church but does not know how many unsaved there are in his community and how best to find lost men and women of the many different segments of society.

What ways of obeying eternal God's command is God blessing? In what segments of society within a few miles of the church building live multitudes of winnable sheep? Many more such questions need to be asked and answered accurately. Leaders of theological education and of denominations must not carry out God's commands blindfolded as to the many situations they face.

Accurate accounts of the multitudinous parts of the human mosaic surrounding us and of the degree to which each part is winnable and has been won can be obtained. Obtaining these will require the addition to most faculties of specialists in effective evangelism and will cost some effort, prayer, and money. Only when we have the picture clearly in front of us can progress be made.

Some years ago I was speaking on church growth to a gathering of ministers in Winnipeg, Manitoba. One of them was the pastor of a bilingual North American Baptist congregation. In 1970 the congregation had been solidly German speaking. It was losing its children and grandchildren who did not speak German. In 1970 the new pastor, therefore, instituted an English service. By 1973, the date of the church growth seminar, two hundred attended the German service and one hundred the English service.

The pastor was deeply touched by the church growth seminar. He came to believe that not only could the children and grandchildren of the German-speaking Baptists be won into an English-speaking church but also that many from two great undiscipled segments of the population in Winnipeg could also be won. Within a mile of the church was a nursing school. Student nurses were largely unchurched. There was also a university community from which few attended any church. None of either group was a member of his church. After 1973 he began a program of effective evangelism in both these segments of society. By 1978, 26 percent of the congregation came from the German-speaking community, 51 percent from the university and nursing communities, and 23 percent from others in the neighborhood.

Once any minister or professor of theology really believes that God wants His lost sons and daughters found and secures accurate information about the individuals and the *ethne* surrounding him, surges of growth may be expected to follow. Each expansion will be different from the others, but each will bring sheaves into the Master's barn. Information as to the exact situation is highly essential in this process.

What Causes Nongrowth, Moderate Growth, and Great Growth?

Essential to our thinking at this point is to realize that knowledge concerning numbers of existing Christians and congregations is only one part of the information needed. Such a picture is a good beginning. It must be followed by knowledge as to what causes nongrowth, moderate growth, and great growth. There will be scores of answers to each of these questions. What causes nongrowth in the inner city will not be the same as what causes nongrowth in the suburbs or a mining community. Once God's command to preach the gospel to all *ethne* leading these *ethne* to faith and obedience has been heard, the courses of action required will vary with every situation. What will work for one person will not necessarily work for others. What will work in one segment of the population may not be nearly so effective in other segments. The degree of education needed by effective pastors and church planters in a population of grade-school graduates will differ from that needed in a population of college graduates. Convinced humanists will need a statement of the unchanging gospel different from the one needed by nominal Christians.

Exact information on all of these topics must be continually sought and taught. This is why five courses on effective evangelism need to be instituted. This is why well-trained specialists in effective evangelism need to be a part of every theological faculty. I hope to see the Bible-believing, Spirit-filled denominations in North America surge ahead. They all have the power. They all hold the great theological convictions. As soon as each of them hears God's commands and enlists in His unswerving purpose, each of them will start growing rapidly.

The hundreds of varieties of church growth (effective evangelism) present different situations. The degree of Christianization in each is different. The receptivity to the gospel in each is different. The problems that must be solved in each are different. The ability and dedication of the workers in each are different. If we are to carry out eternal God's command effectively, we must have accurate information about all these aspects of each segment of the population.

Since theological schools are preparing pastors who will be able to assemble and use the many kinds of exact information of which I have been speaking, it is obvious that much more than one four-hour elective on evangelism is needed. If the pastors and ministers from seminaries of the world are to operate in the light of exact knowledge concerning the multitudinous segments of the population to be won, several four-hour courses will be needed. These required courses on effective evangelism must very soon become a part of the curricula of all schools of theological education.

13

Church Growth
by Clergy or Laity?

Is effective evangelism of non-Christians the work of clergy or laity? Does the minister alone determine whether his congregation finds and folds the lost in its vicinity? Is his task to do the job himself or to train his members to do it? Should this book be read only by the clergy or also by the laity? These are most important questions for every Bible college, seminary, and denomination. Let me lay before you some striking illustrations.

Pastor Paul Yonggi Cho in 1958

The most dramatic illustration of church growth in the world today comes from the Full Gospel Church on Yoido Island, a suburb of Seoul, Korea. Under the able leadership of Dr. Paul Yonggi Cho, its minister, this Assemblies of God congregation has grown from two thousand in 1958 to four hundred thousand today. The two thousand met in a large tent in the bombed and flattened heart of the great city of Seoul. The four hundred thousand meet in a very large and beautiful church and in thousands of house churches scattered across the entire urban area. God used Pastor Yonggi Cho alone to gather the first two thousand. His tireless work, his Spirit-filled dynamism, and his unceasing prayer brought together a congregation that grew from a couple of hundred to a couple of thousand in three years. Then Pastor Cho suffered nervous exhaustion. His physician assured him he would never preach again. He was confined to his bed.

Nevertheless, he called in a hundred of his most devout members. They filled the room where he lay on a cot. He said to them "The care of this congregation now rests on you. Each one of you must gather the twenty or so members of this church who live in his or her immediate neighborhood for a meeting of prayer and Bible study every week and must see that they come to this tent for Sunday worship."

The hundred members instantly protested that they were very ordinary people and had neither the ability nor the biblical knowledge to do this. He replied, "God will give you the ability. You can love the twenty people who form your congregation, your house church. The members of your house church live in intimate contact with many non-Christians in this vast urban complex. Your members can demonstrate the new love, justice, and kind way of life you now practice and can win many of the non-Christians to Christ."

God healed Yonggi Cho, and he was back in his pulpit within a month. The hundred house churches prospered. They soon became two hundred, then four hundred, then six hundred. Yonggi Cho, with some help from the American Assemblies of God, built the largest church building in Korea. Its main auditorium seated eight thousand worshipers. A television placed on the enormous pulpit showed him another thousand gathered in the great hall below the auditorium. These thousand also saw and heard the preacher via closed-circuit television. Thus every Sunday Yonggi Cho spoke to nine thousand people. He soon found that he had to have four services—at 9, 10:30, 2, and 4 o'clock.

In 1974 I addressed nine thousand people at the second service on that Sunday. There were two more such services. In all, thirty-six thousand members attended church that day.

After the service, I was greatly impressed with five large offices below the auditorium. Each was filled with filing cabinets, which contained a card for each of the thirty-six thousand baptized believers of the church. In the filing cabinets the members were grouped according to the eighteen hundred house churches then in existence. Every one of the eighteen hundred house churches or cells sent its leader to meet every Wednesday night with Yonggi Cho and his helpers for a couple of hours. I asked Pastor Cho who these lay leaders were. Were they doctors, lawyers, teachers, and other such people?

"Oh no," replied Pastor Cho, "those people are far too busy. The eighteen hundred who gather here are very ordinary citizens, but they love and care for their small house churches. They know each member individually, and they lead them in prayer and Bible study."

I thought immediately of the tremendous growth of the New Testament church led not by rabbis, scribes, and doctors of the law, but by fishermen, tax gatherers, and many unnamed and ordinary men in hundreds of small gatherings meeting at houses, patios, gardens, and a few years later in catacombs. The first answer to the question posed by the title of this chapter is that effective evangelization is carried on by a joint effort by pastor and people. In it the pastor performs a small and very important percentage of the total work. The people perform a large and important percentage. If any denomination or congregation today wishes to become effective in its proclamation of the gospel, it must inspire and organize a substantial number of its men and women to become ardent and well-trained lay evangelists.

John Wesley and Class Meetings

What happened in Korea between 1958 and 1985, twenty-seven years, has happened again and again throughout history. A most dramatic illustration is provided by John Wesley, an Anglican clergymen two hundred years ago. As he sought to revive the millions of nominal Christians in England, Scotland, Ireland, and Wales, he came to the conclusion that it could be done only by organizing class meetings led by committed Christian men. Few if any of these had theological training or were seminary graduates. All, however, were committed Christians. He provided for them the guidelines according to which they were to reach out to the unsaved, win the unsaved, teach the unsaved, and lead them into committed, prayerful Christian life.

In his book, *To Spread the Power*, Dr. George Hunter tells in considerable detail of Wesley's methods. He emphasizes that Wesley operated according to the principles that the church growth movement is emphasizing today. Wesley did not call these "church growth" principles, but that is what they were. If he had not emphasized these methods, his movement would not have grown and grown until today there are more than 40 million Methodists scattered around the world.

The training of committed Christians to find and nurture their unsaved brothers and sisters, neighbors and friends, is a key to growth needed by every ordained pastor. The fact that so few pastors use this key is very largely responsible for the static condition of many denominations. How to train laymen, of course, varies from congregation to congregation. Consequently, Bible colleges and seminaries must teach a four-hour course detailing the many different ways of instructing the laity. This key to obeying eternal God's command can be seized by the ordained leaders of all congregations in all parts of the globe. What a tremendous and effective army will be found, organized, trained, and set to work as leaders of the church grasp this truth and act upon it!

Illiterate Preachers and Baptist Multiplication

Of considerable significance is the fact that, while at the time of the Revolutionary War the large denominations in the United States were the Episcopalian, Presbyterian, and Congregational, by 1976 (two hundred years later) the large denominations were the Methodists and the Baptists. The Episcopalians, Presbyterians, Congregationalists, and Lutherans had, of course, grown but not nearly so much as the Methodists and Baptists.

Why was this so? There are many reasons. But one, concerning which there can be little doubt, is that the slow-growing denominations rely for their growth very largely upon well-trained ministers, whereas the Methodists, with their class meetings, which soon become congregations, and the Baptists frequently used Spirit-filled people who had relatively little formal education. As one reads the history of the rapid expansion of Baptist churches, he runs across instances of men of very little formal education. These, filled with the Holy Spirit and reading the Bible through from cover to cover, became effective proclaimers of the Word to those frontier people, among which were many actually illiterate men and women. Indeed, I read of more than one Baptist who was illiterate when he married. His wife taught him to read. Later after his conversion he became an able preacher.

Be assured that I am not advocating scant training for ministers. Fuller Theological Seminary and the School of World Mission emphasize the need for abundant instruction and education of prospective ministers and missionaries. It does need to be said, however, that there is a danger that highly educated men will not be heard by large segments of the population. If effective evangelism is left solely to the highly educated, millions of the women and men living around us will not listen to what we have to say. This is one reason why ordained ministers must enlist and train at least 10 percent of their members to become effective evangelists. These members of their churches will speak to their neighbors and friends in ways that vary from neighborhood to neighborhood. They will be heard exactly as were the unlearned apostles in the early church.

Evangelistic Home Bible Studies in Boston

A good illustration comes from the city of Boston. There a Church of Christ minister, Kip McKean, in 1978 came to a small congregation of about fifty members. By 1983, five years later, this had grown to a congregation of fourteen hundred baptized believers. As I corresponded with Pastor McKean, he gave several reasons for this amazing growth. Among them was the fact that every week that congregation of fourteen hundred members assembled in 150— repeat, 150—evangelistic home Bible studies. These met in 150 parts of the great city of Boston.

To be counted as an *evangelistic* home Bible study, each had to have as many nonmembers attend as Christians. "If just the saints of God gather to study the Bible," wrote Pastor McKean, "the meeting has very little evangelistic potency. If, however, believers and nonbelievers, members and nonmembers meet, faith flows from believers to nonbelievers in a remarkable fashion." To be sure, the Bible study course that all these groups employed was carefully designed to meet the conditions of modern life in a great city and to present the Christian alternatives. The pastor never visited these evangelistic home Bible studies. There the faith was communicated by the Holy Spirit through the laity.

Another illustration comes from a recent church growth seminar held in a great southern city. An Episcopal rector at the close of one of the sessions said, "This city is divided by a railway which runs through it. On this side live the whites. On that side live the blacks and other minorities. On that side of the tracks there is not a single Episcopal church. I have recently had close contact with a wonderful Christian from that side of the tracks. He is not a seminary graduate. I am going to encourage and help him to start an Episcopal church on that side of the tracks. We ought to have several Episcopal churches down there."

Creating a Core of
Effective Evangelists in Your Congregation

In every seminary and Bible college are gathered students and professors who every Sunday will play leading parts in many congregations. All these face a general population in which are multitudes of humanists, secularists, materialists, and nominal and lapsed Christians of many denominations from Roman Catholic to Pentecostal. Most of the congregations will be either little-growing or nongrowing; some will be declining. The record of their growth over the past twenty years will abundantly prove this. Could these congregations be turned around? Could they become like Pastor Yonggi Cho's great congregation in Korea or like Pastor McKean's congregation in Boston?

The answer to this question must be carefully framed. If we were to select the right people in each congregation, train them, work with them, encourage them, pray with them, and help them, we would beyond doubt be able to turn many nongrowing churches around. We would beyond question start many vigorous Spirit-filled house churches. On the other hand, in some congregations, no matter how much we tried, we could not find the right people. Possibly this would be due to the way we went about it. Possibly this would be due to decades of belief that all such work is the work of the pastor. He is paid to do it. Why should we do it?

Nevertheless, I trust that as Bible colleges and seminaries establish many required courses on effective evangelism, many of their graduates will create bands of laymen or laywomen who will be effective evangelists. These will start evangelistic home Bible studies. They will learn how to speak winningly and effectively to their neighbors and friends. All across America congregation after congregation, presbytery after presbytery, union after union are wakening to the multitudes of the unreached and to eternal God's command to disciple them. The ways in which they obey this command will be multitudinous. The effectiveness of each unit will vary. But that the total will be impressive is hard to doubt.

14

The Heart of
Today's Opportunity

Theological seminaries, divinity schools, and Bible schools can unquestionably play a significant part in the evangelization of the United States and all other nations.

As theological training schools begin to see the *theological necessity* that all congregations carry on effective evangelism, great growth will certainly follow. As theological training schools see the enormous numbers of the unreached in today's and tomorrow's world, they will educate their students in effective evangelism.

They will recognize the vast nominality that characterizes so many of today's church members. They will not close their eyes to the tidal wave of secularism, materialism, and nominalism that has swept over the Western world and all the branches of its church. The need for revival and renewal within the church, resulting in a great multiplication of living, Spirit-filled congregations, will dominate their thinking. Church growth at home and abroad will become one of their principal emphases.

Faculties in theological schools ought to take most seriously those Greek words *ta ethne* found so frequently in the New Testament. Faculties will increasingly realize that they are surrounded at home and abroad by thousands of these ethnic units, segments of society, unreached peoples—pieces of the vast urban and rural mosaics. *Matheteusate panta ta ethne* (Matt. 28:19) will be heard as the command—not the suggestion or request—of the ultimate Authority of the universe.

Seminaries will recoil from the concept that really Christian congregations can be satisfied merely to maintain themselves, pay their pastors well, worship in beautiful buildings, and hear interesting sermons.

Agreeing that every truly Christian congregation controlled by the Holy Spirit will surge out to seek God's lost children—whether these are non-Christians or nominal Christians—and bring them home, seminaries and Bible colleges will develop at least five four-hour courses teaching effective evangelization of every segment of the exceedingly complex modern society. They will require that all students take these courses. They will recruit faculty members who have a burden for effective evangelization. They will inaugurate a truly Christian response to the most receptive world ever to exist. They will begin a mighty multiplication of soundly Christian, increasingly just, and brotherly congregations in every *ethnos*, tribe, tongue, and people in their own nation and every other nation.

They will do all this as an essential part of adequate and effective ministerial education.

Afterword

Pastor-Evangelists: Need of the Hour Everywhere

Roger S. Greenway, former Professor of Missions and Gospel Communications at Westminster Theological Seminary and now Executive Director of Christian Reformed World Ministries, has edited a most interesting book, *The Pastor-Evangelist*.* In it he and twelve co-authors have fascinatingly described the many evangelistic opportunities facing all pastors in all branches of the universal church. Dr. Greenway and his collaborators portray in a most interesting way the incidents and principles that underlie every pastor's life. Many quotations from the great leaders of the church make delightful reading.

Dr. Greenway does not argue that theological seminaries should require every ministerial candidate to take five courses on evangelism. He does, however, present truthfully the evangelistic challenges and opportunities every pastor faces. Readers will see the tremendous need for students in theological seminaries to become capable of presenting Christ effectively in hundreds of everyday situations.

The following chapter by Dr. Greenway is excerpted from *The Pastor-Evangelist*, pages 182-200, and is reprinted by permission. Read this delightful chapter and walk in its light.

---

* *The Pastor-Evangelist: Preacher, Model, and Mobilizer for Church Growth* (Phillipsburg, N.J.: Presbyterian and Reformed, 1987).

At the meetings of the Consultation on World Evangelization held in Thailand in 1980, George Peters, who for many years taught Missions at Dallas Theological Seminary, made several pointed comments about pastors and evangelism. He talked about the churches of Europe, where in his retirement Peters made annual visits addressing pastors and furloughing missionaries. Peters told us that he had recently addressed a gathering of 350 European pastors, all of them conservative in their theology. He asked them how many had ever studied evangelism. Only five said that they had taken a course in the subject. Twenty had attended at least a one-day workshop in evangelism. The vast majority had never received any formal instruction on how to do or organize evangelism. Was there any connection, Peters asked, between this lack of training and the major complaint throughout Europe that the churches weren't growing? His own analysis was that the "European churches and their leaders have never seen the connection between evangelism and pastoral ministry."

My own observations in other parts of the world bear out what George Peters said. When churches fail to present the claims of Christ evangelistically to the unsaved world, a series of things happen. The gospel of God's saving grace no longer glows in pulpit and pew as it formerly did, and members slip away. Among the remnant, religious energies are directed toward other things, usually social issues and human development. Theologians add to the process by providing a conceptual framework of soteriological universalism that does not require personal conversion and thereby excludes biblical evangelism. Evangelism, in fact, is redefined as social action. As far as the churches are concerned, it is a downward spiral as unevangelistic leaders produce unevangelistic institutions, which in turn produce a body of people whose religious impulses go in many directions, carrying some of them even to distant parts of the world, doing many commendable things but lacking evangelistic motivation and power. Such workers cannot produce growing churches. Though pastors are not the whole problem, they certainly are a key part of it. And, I would add, they can also be the catalysts who turn the spiral around.

George Peters made a second statement about the strategy mission agencies follow around the world: "I've just come back from a round-the-world tour of mission fields on behalf of several major boards, and I'm disgusted. I've seen a thousand small, stagnant churches that aren't going anywhere. I told the mission executives they had better stop emphasizing church planting until they've learned to make churches grow. The pastors don't know how to evangelize and the churches just hang on with a handful of members."

One of the dismal realities we don't talk about in mission literature, particularly literature of a promotional kind, is that we have planted a lot of churches that are as evangelistically sterile as many of our older churches in the West. Nongrowing churches in places where receptivity to the gospel is generally high is an unresolved dilemma, and I believe God has raised up the pentecostal churches partly as an indictment of the older denominations. The evangelistic sterility of mainline churches, including some that remain orthodox in their doctrine, is a terrible witness to Christianity and in my opinion stands at the top of the list of the problems we face in world evangelization.

My thesis is that the solution begins with the pastors who lead the congregations and the training they receive for ministry. Many years ago, the great missionary statesman John R. Mott expressed this truth succinctly:

> The secret of enabling the church to press forward in the non-Christian world is one of leadership. The people do not go

beyond their leaders in knowledge and zeal, nor surpass them
in consecration and sacrifice. The Christian pastor . . . holds
the divinely appointed office for inspiring and guiding the
thought and activities of the church. By virtue of his position he
can be a mighty force in the world's evangelization.

In the first chapter of this book I said that the pastor's responsibility in regard to evangelism is threefold. He must teach and preach
evangelism from the Word of God, building a solid basis of understanding and commitment within the congregation. He must model
evangelism in his own life and ministry, teaching by example and
guiding others in the process. Finally, the pastor must mobilize the
membership in ways that put feet to doctrine and theory. His role is
that of organizer, equipper, and catalyst. Under his leadership the
members explore new possibilities for reaching their community
and incorporate evangelism into every department of church life.

Much of the book has dealt with ways this can be done, and my
purpose in this final chapter is to highlight certain issues and review
the general framework of pastoral evangelism. I include a number of
illustrations of pastoral evangelism in action, building around the
three pivotal areas of modeling, teaching, and organizing. In response to the possible accusation that I have been unduly hard on
pastors, I begin with some thoughts in their defense, things that
need to be said though they imply a degree of admonishment.

In Defense of the Average Pastor

First, something needs to be said about para-church organizations that specialize in evangelism and whose record in gaining
converts frequently exceeds that of the established church. At the
Consultation in Thailand, I heard pastors from various parts of the
world complain that they felt they were being victimized in the eyes
of their people. Pastors, they complained, always get the blame
when the church compares poorly with highly charged efforts of
para-church mission agencies. Often the members themselves, or
the circumstances in which the church is located and working,
inhibit the kind of growth people demand. The pastors gathered in
Thailand pointed out also that para-church organizations generally

are structured differently from the church. Their main intent is missionary service and outreach, whereas pastors and churches have a host of additional responsibilities besides evangelism. Workers in para-church mission agencies generally don't have to counsel troubled families, conduct funerals, teach ladies societies, and comfort the sick and elderly. They can focus on the purpose for which they are organized and maintained, evangelism. If their success in that department seems to exceed that of the average pastor and the institutional church, the reasons are obvious.

The pastors' complaint is legitimate, and critics of the church need to be reminded that the ministries of the church go far beyond the specialized concerns of para-church organizations. They must remember, too, that the task of evangelism is not completed when people become believers. Discipleship is a long ongoing process, involving years of instruction, guidance, and discipline. Without churches to do this, what would become of the fruits of the para-church activities? The need, as I see it, is for church and para-church institutions to work together more closely, to integrate their efforts and avoid all semblance of competition and leadership stealing. *I maintain the conviction that, when the local church enjoys the leadership of pastors committed to evangelism, it takes a back seat to no other organization in drawing sinners to Christ and nurturing them over the long haul to faithful and responsible discipleship.*

Second, I defend those pastors who serve in difficult locations. There are rural communities where many residents have departed and few young people stay around. Pastors in declining communities see many of the talented people leaving, and they easily become frustrated and discouraged because all the exciting places of ministry seem to be somewhere else. Then there are inner city neighborhoods where people's lives are, in varying degrees, shattered and torn apart by sin and its consequences. Numerical growth is slow, and pastors spend much of their time healing wounds and holding members together against a withering barrage of negative forces. Some churches are located in places where they are cut off from the mainstream because of language or cultural differences, and yet the remnant is there and requires pastoral care.

Highly favorable locations can also be deceptive. There are communities so favorable that almost any church will grow, even without evangelism. In North America and Europe these usually are suburban locations where large numbers of middle-class families are moving in and can be counted on to join an evangelical church. Church planters rely heavily on demographic studies to determine where these high potential locations are likely to develop, and they shape their strategy accordingly. From a practical standpoint this makes sense, and many of the highly acclaimed churches in America are built in this way. But the strategy, especially if it is followed to the exclusion of all others, has some serious drawbacks. It may represent the planned neglect of urban neighborhoods where large numbers of people need to be evangelized and pastored. It tends to focus entirely on "our kind" of people, to the neglect of social and ethnic minorities. It may say in effect that the only churches worth planting and pastoring are those which promise, in businessmen's fashion, a "high return" on the investment. Therefore, in defense of some "low yield" pastorates I raise this word of caution. *God's people are found in many different locations and circumstances, and all of them need mission-hearted pastors. Heaven will reward many who receive no laurels on earth. Let us not look down on those less-fertile fields, but honor the laborers for their perseverance.*

Third, in defense of pastors who feel frustrated over evangelism something needs to be said about the Christian colleges and seminaries that fail to provide adequate training in this area. What George Peters observed in the case of European-educated pastors is also true of schooling on this side of the Atlantic and in many Third World institutions. Most courses in missions and evangelism are heavy on theory but terribly light on practice, and some graduates have never studied evangelism at all. Courses in the department of practical theology traditionally are oriented toward the internal needs of congregations and not toward the evangelization of the unsaved outside. It is no wonder, therefore, that pastors feel frustrated when churches decline and evangelism-minded lay people look elsewhere for direction. *Evangelism tends to have the same importance and place in the churches that it has in the seminaries, and for that reason our concern for evangelism through local churches carries us to the schools where church leadership is formed.*

Few people have known more about seminaries around the world and how well they succeed in producing pastor-evangelists than James F. Hopewell, associated as he was with the Theological Education Fund from its beginning in 1958, long before it had formal connection with the World Council of Churches and its viewpoint. Hopewell visited hundreds of theological institutions around the world with the specific purpose of cutting through the outer, superficial appearances and getting at the core of their mission and ministry. Defining "mission" as the witness Christians make outside the normal frontiers of the church, and "candidate" as the person being prepared by some theological institution for a career in Christian service, Hopewell said the following:

> The problem is that surprisingly few candidates are prepared to engage in that mission with any consistency or accuracy. And while this fault may be attributed to most any aspect of modern church structure, it seems particularly encouraged by the pattern of theological education now practiced in most seminaries around the world. . . .

> Now I would like to contend . . . that most of these factors that comprise our understanding of typical theological education have been unconsciously designed to avoid, and therefore to hinder, the basic Christian intention of mission. And I do not mean to beat the anti-intellectual drum against higher learning. What rather concerns an increasing number of critics is that the very tool of higher learning has been misappropriated to perform a third-rate job for a second-rate church structure. In a time when our understanding of the ministry more and more implies its dynamic, missionary function, we continue to rely upon a system of preparation which at its roots is essentially static and isolationist.[1]

In view of the increased pressure building up today for leadership that knows how to evangelize, I predict that Christian colleges and seminaries will have to revamp their programs or face decline. The realities of a world in which the percentage of unchurched and unsaved people rises every year demand that church leadership be

1. James F. Hopewell, "Preparing the Candidate for Mission," *International Review of Missions* 56:158-63.

trained in new ways to meet the challenge. *Evangelism must be returned to its rightful place in the classroom and in the church, or the trend toward para-churchism will become a stampede.*

Certain readers may want to challenge this, and therefore I invite them to reflect on the following. A well-known evangelical seminary that has always stood for scholarship and doctrinal conservatism recently sent a questionnaire to its alumni asking them to rank the courses they felt had been the most helpful in preparing them for pastoral ministry. As reported by the pastors, the top five were church history, Greek, Hebrew, systematics, and biblical theology. At or near the bottom were preaching, evangelism, and church growth. Another questionnaire was sent to the elders and lay leaders of the churches being served by the seminary's graduates. They were asked to indicate the chief *weaknesses* they observed in pastors. Surprise! The top three weaknesses were in communication, preaching, and evangelism, areas that lie at the exact opposite of the "most helpful" courses identified by the pastors. That seminary, and many similar institutions, really has something to think about. The discrepancy in responses may reflect the quality of the teaching in the respective departments. In addition, it reflects a profound difference of perception between scholars and church members as to what people in the pew are looking for in their leaders. Certainly the members had detected certain deficiencies in the training received by their pastors, and they were outspoken in their desire to see the gaps filled. That particular seminary is taking serious steps to shore up its weaknesses, and I hope all pastor-training institutions will take warning.

Areas in Which Pastors Preach and Teach Evangelism

Responsibility for equipping members for kingdom service and evangelism lies with the pastors, the spiritual leaders of God's people. The biblical pattern is teaching, modeling, and organizing. In teaching I include Sunday preaching, which in most churches is the chief didactic instrument. Unless the pastor's teaching-preaching sounds forth the gospel and creates the atmosphere of evangelism in the church, it is unlikely that the church will become mobilized for effective outreach.

Members must be able to expect that in every worship service the good news of hope and salvation through Christ will be heard in such a manner that children, youth, and the casual visitor will be able to grasp something of its meaning. Unfortunately, this is not the case in every church. Some time ago I was talking with an elder from a large Reformed congregation. I know the pastor of that church well, and he is a gifted speaker and deeply committed to the orthodox expression of the faith. The elder, a man of long-standing leadership in the church, related to me how he and his wife had witnessed by word and deed for many years to his unchurched neighbors. Repeatedly they had invited the couple to attend church, but they had always refused. Finally, they agreed to go just once. "My wife and I took them to the pentecostal church," said the elder. Surprised, I asked him why they had not taken them to their own church. "Well, you know how it is in our church," he replied. "Our preacher is great, but he's usually very deep, and we were afraid they wouldn't hear the gospel."

That was an awful indictment on the elder's church and its pulpit ministry. It sheds light also on the fact that that particular church has sent scores of members into para-church ministries, all of them perfectly legitimate in themselves but not contributing in any direct way to the growth of the congregation. Various attempts over the years were made by the church to develop an effective outreach program, but nothing seemed to work. The church kept nourishing the faith of its members, many of whom went off to engage in evangelistic ministries through outside organizations, while the church hardly drew a new member except through its own children, occasional transfers, and a few marriages.

The preaching of sound doctrine without a burning heart for evangelism is as unbiblical as it is dangerous. Likewise are pastoral prayers without tears for lost souls. The evangelistic tone of the congregation is set on Sunday where the passion of the pastor's heart becomes evident and is transmitted to the members. In a sermon entitled "Without Christ—Nothing" Charles H. Spurgeon said the following:

> You may have sound doctrine, and yet do nothing unless you have Christ *in your spirit*. I have known all the doctrines of grace

to be unmistakably preached, and yet there have been no conversions; for this reason, that they were not expected and scarcely desired. In former years many orthodox preachers thought it to be their sole duty to comfort and confirm the godly few who by dint of great perseverance found out the holes and corners in which they prophesied. These brethren spoke of sinners as of people whom God might possibly gather in if he thought fit to do so; but they did not care much whether he did so or not. As to weeping over sinners as Christ wept over Jerusalem; as to venturing to invite them to Christ as the Lord did when he stretched out his hands all the day long; as to lamenting with Jeremiah over a perishing people, they had no sympathy with such emotions and feared that they savoured of Arminianism. Both preacher and congregation were cased in a hard shell, and lived as if their own salvation was the sole design of their existence. If anybody did grow zealous and seek conversions, straightway they said he was indiscreet, or conceited. When a church falls into this condition it is, as to its spirit, "without Christ." What comes of it? Some of you know by your own observation what does come of it. The comfortable corporation exists and grows for a little while, but it comes to nothing in the long run; and so it must: there can be no fruit-bearing where there is not the spirit of Christ as well as the doctrine of Christ. Except the spirit of the Lord rest upon you, causing you to agonize for the salvation of men even as Jesus did, ye can do nothing.[2]

Spurgeon spoke directly to the point, and the only corrective for the "comfortable corporation" is to be led by pastors who have the heart of the Great Pastor, Jesus. His heart must increasingly become ours so that His ministry may shine through us. Preachers and churches without Christ's spirit of compassion for the lost have always been around. They display certain strengths for a while, even a long while, but eventually they divide, dwindle, and close down unless they repent and return to the spirit of the Lord. In our day we see how thousands of renewed Christians spend their energies on ministries apart from the organized churches mainly because of this condition.

2. Charles H. Spurgeon, *Sermons on Revival* (Grand Rapids: Zondervan, 1958), pp. 187-88.

Worship and preaching stand at the core of congregational life. Whenever churches have growth problems, you can be certain something is wrong with their worship life. On the other hand, preaching that is biblical, intelligible, winsome, and delivered in the power of the Holy Spirit sets churches on fire and sends members into the streets charged with enthusiasm to draw others in.

Lyle E. Schaller, whose writings about the church and the ministry every pastor should devour, has given what he calls the "Seven Earmarks of Growing Churches." In an article that appeared in *Second Monday*, May 1981, Schaller says that churches that grow successfully through evangelism are characterized by the following elements, which I have slightly recast:

1. *Biblical Preaching.* To the surprise of many church members, says Schaller, more people on the outside are looking for good biblical preaching than we generally assume. They will come to a church where the preacher delivers an authentic word from the Lord and applies Scripture to the real needs of today. I will say more about this point later.

2. *Emphasis on Evangelism.* In growing churches, evangelism is not left for the pastor or a few "mission enthusiasts." Such churches have a cadre of unpaid lay evangelists who are motivated by what they hear from the pulpit to go out and win others to Christ.

3. *Strong Emphasis on Fellowship.* Whereas in most traditional churches the membership circle is larger than the fellowship circle because a percentage of members do not get involved and never become active, the growing churches have a fellowship circle that is larger than the membership circle. Outsiders are continually being drawn toward Christ and His church by the services and activities of the congregation.

4. *Opportunites to Express Commitment.* Schaller says that growing churches recognize that different people have different gifts and different needs, and these churches intentionally present a wide variety of opportunities for members to affirm their faith, even in its early stages, and express their commitment through the church. When churches have only narrow programs and stifle creative ex-

pression, the gifts and talents of many members remain unused, or people go elsewhere to express their commitment. Such churches neither meet needs nor grow.

5. *Openness to New Leadership.* Growing churches take advantage of new leaders that come into the fellowship from outside the original "church family." Nongrowing churches, however, keep the key leadership positions for people belonging to the "mainline families" that have run the church for a generation or more. A high percentage of churches fall into this category.

6. *Specialties in Ministry.* Churches that continue to draw newcomers into their fellowship are churches that, in addition to the basic ministries found in all congregations, focus on special ministries for which they become well known. These ministries are person-centered, are designed to meet particular needs, intentionally include an evangelistic dimension, and offer church members fresh opportunities to express their gifts and interests.

7. *A Pastor Who Likes People.* Surprisingly enough, not all pastors like people, and it shows. Some pastors prefer books and the solitude of their private studies to the topsy-turvy world of interpersonal relationships and bleeding people. They may be highly trained and skilled in professional ways, but they lack the essential ingredient of love for people.

I was called in once by the pastor of a large Presbyterian church in Mexico City to help him assess what was wrong in the Sunday school. The Sunday school director was highly educated, a professor in the denominational seminary, and he seemed to have everything organized very well. In fact, he took his position in the Sunday school very seriously and chose the best curriculum. After a long talk with him, however, I discovered what the problem was. He realized it himself, and admitted, "I love organizing and directing the Sunday school, but I hate kids." The pupils felt it, the teachers chafed under his leadership, and the whole program suffered. I wonder how many stagnant churches suffer from the same problem.

Returning to point one of Schaller's list of growth characteristics, we note that quality biblical preaching is absolutely essential.

Preaching and Sunday worship set the tone for the whole life of the congregation. What happens on Sunday is the key. Here the character of the church is formed, directions are set, visions are shared, and the Spirit through the Word moves the church in one direction or another. Romans 10:17, a text that years ago I chose as the theme text of my pastoral and missionary ministry, is the clue to it all: "Faith comes from hearing the message, and the message is heard through the word of Christ." Good biblical preaching builds Christians and makes churches grow, and this is the pastor's foremost task. Edgar Whitaker Work expressed it this way:

> Courage in the ministry is a contagious spirit felt by others. When men preach in this spirit their preaching has a power of appeal that grips souls. You catch it in the way they use the Bible. You feel the strong word of truth coming to you as you listen to sermons of this kind. Circumlocutions give way. Direct, positive ways of speech take their place. Plain, simple, straightforward utterance in the Gospel wins attention. Men feel the ribs and structure of the Gospel. Again and again the preacher who is bold and outspoken in these ways makes irresistible use of his text. He thrusts it, as it were, beyond the mind, into the heart. He gives it imperative force with his hearers. They *must* hear, he will not let them close their ears.[3]

Modeling—Test of the Preacher's Grit and Integrity

Good preaching, however, does not stand alone. It must be in combination with the whole ministry of the pastor and the life of the church. This principle has been reiterated in various ways throughout the book.

Vincent Taylor once said that the test of any theologian is, Can he write a tract? Taylor was not interested in any kind of theology that did not help to evangelize. I would add another question: Can the titan in the pulpit lead one soul, in private, to Christ? It is one thing to deliver a fine sermon, and still another to take the message to the street, the sick room, and the house of mourning. These occasions occur over and over again in the normal routine of pastoring, and it

---

3. Edgar Whitaker Work, *Every Minister His Own Evangelist* (Fleming, 1927), p. 125.

is in these day-by-day situations that the pastor becomes the model for the congregation. The members can be depended on to take notice.

Pastoral visitation, particularly in homes and hospitals, is a key to success in ministry and evangelism. When churches become stagnant and membership drops off, it is usually the case that the pastors and the elders have not been calling on the people. When it comes to visitation, there is little difference between the work of the local pastor and the work of the home or foreign missionary. Both require aggressive pursuit of people. A Presbyterian pastor in Canada told me recently what had happened in one of the large churches in Toronto. "The pastors didn't think visiting was part of their job," he said. "They didn't even visit the families of the Kirk session, and as a result the elders didn't visit either. The ministers had the idea that if members needed help, they'd come on their own, and the minister didn't have to go out looking for them." The church he was describing was once one of Toronto's finest, but today it stands almost empty.

Visitation evangelism is one of the great needs of the hour. Some sixty million people in this country are classified as "unchurched." That is, they are not members of a church, nor have they attended religious services for a six-month period except for religious holidays. Many of them are not hostile to the Christian religion, and they show interest in religious subjects. They buy many religious books, including the Bible. What keeps them from joining the community of active believers? One basic reason is that they have not been personally invited to do so. Many pastors and congregations are neglecting the fundamental step of going out after people and inviting them to attend the place of worship. Coupled with this is the need for evidence of pastoral concern and availability. Unchurched people generally have notions about organized religion and about clergymen in particular, which can only be dismissed through pastoral visitation. Pastors need to seek out every possible opportunity to talk to unchurched people about spiritual matters and dispel by personal word and example the false notions outsiders have about churches. In actuality, pastors by virtue of their office and the respect in which they are held in the community, have tremendous advantages when making calls. Pastors are the last professionals to make home visits, and seldom do they have a door slammed in their faces. And if they do, so what? They are then in good company, for Jesus was "despised and rejected of men" for their salvation.

I used to tell my students in the Juan Calvino Seminary in Mexico City that there were two pieces of leather they must expect to wear out if they wanted to plant churches and see them grow—the leather around their Bibles and on the soles of their shoes. One student took this advice seriously, and when he told me that the church to which he had been assigned over summer break had doubled in size, he added, "And maestro, I wore out three pairs of shoes!" He hardly needed to tell me, because churches seldom grow without a great deal of visitation. The concern the pastor shows in the time he spends calling becomes the model for the members of the congregation in their concern for one another and for outsiders. There is simply no substitute for the pastor's visits, in the home, the hospital, and wherever people are found.

Furthermore, it is excellent therapy for pastors to engage regularly in direct evangelism on strange and unfriendly turf. They need to face the same world ordinary church members confront day after day. Away from the security of the pulpit and church building pastors should expose themselves to hostile ridicule, barbed questions, and instant rejection. Jesus exposed Himself in that way, and we should not avoid it.

In the rough and tumble of the world the evangelizing pastor gains fresh insights into the non-Christian mind. When hecklers in a prison block, a campus gathering, or the open street challenge his religious assertions, he learns new things about human depravity and the harsh realities of evangelism. He finds what it takes to prepare and preach evangelistic messages without the use of familiar clichés and the religious background we tend to take for granted in the church. In my own ministry, some of the hardest messages I ever preached were in the open air before a mixed audience of Buddhists and Hindus, where anything, including violence, might be expected. And I never felt closer to the ministry of Jesus, who seldom enjoyed safe turf and was a street preacher who made

Himself vulnerable to hostile listeners.

More important than formal study is prayer. It takes a lot for a teacher of homiletics to say that, but I do. When the pastor has a passion for souls, it shines through in everything he does and says, especially his prayers in private and before the congregation. Parishioners who breathe an atmosphere charged by evangelistic passion conveyed through the pastor's sermons and prayers, and attested by his ministry among them and their neighbors, eventually partake of the same spirit. It grows on them, and they touch others. Their prayers echo his, and his ministry carries over into theirs. As Edgar Whitaker Work stated it, "The minister's own practice of prayer will have much to do with the evangelistic force of his sermons. If his sermon is based in prayer in the making of it, if he rises from his knees to go to the pulpit, a power goes with the sermon that opens the way to the hearts of men. Prayer as a background to preaching is a condition that we can little understand, and certainly cannot measure. Men of power in prayer cannot preach a sermon, no matter what the subject, without making it evangelistic."[4] Prayer makes the preacher, and prayer makes the pastor. Men of great prayer for the lost and straying turn churches into power-houses of evangelism.

Organizing the Church for Evangelism

Some pastors have special gifts in evangelism. Many do not. But all pastors have the responsibility to facilitate evangelism in and through their congregations. Pastoral leadership in evangelism extends from the pulpit and classroom to the people in the pew who are moved to action by the Word and the Spirit and encouraged by the pastor's interest and example. There is one step more, and it extends to the structures and programs of the church, including new ones created intentionally with outreach in mind.

In this area it is especially helpful to define clearly the target people. In one church I pastored we spelled out repeatedly to the congregation that in the geographical area around the church we

4. Work, pp. 41-43.

were aiming our evangelism program toward the "unsaved, un-churched, and uncared-for." There were plenty of people in all three categories. Some had a flimsy church connection but knew nothing of personal salvation through Christ. We worked through the Sunday school, youth organizations, and a chain of midweek evangelistic home Bible studies to reach them. Some of our neighbors had never been connected to any church. We found that a midweek women's program held at church and focused on fellowship and Bible study proved to be one of the most fruitful things we did to reach the unchurched. The physically and spiritually uncared-for were all around us, and the deacons were mobilized to respond to appeals for help, especially food, and to tie in their ministry with the overall evangelistic thrust of the church.

Physical and emotional needs are seldom found in isolation from spiritual needs, and evangelistic deacons are a church's vital link to a neighborhood where there are poor, troubled, and unsaved people. Pastors should have no fear of social ministries so long as they are not given a higher priority than the spiritual. In the past, mainline denominations went wrong at the point when social service was given a higher priority than evangelism. Churches stopped their former activities in evangelism and spiritual outreach and shifted to social service as their main concern. That shift precipitated the downward spiral of those churches and denominations.

In organizing a church for evangelism, therefore, the key factor is to work out what you believe to be the biblical priorities and then hang on to them tenaciously as you develop the program. The relation of the ministries of evangelism and social service is crucial, and in a biblically directed church it will not be a question of *either . . . or*, but of *both . . . and*. Evangelical churches can grow and keep growing when they emphasize soul-saving, life-transforming evangelism, and the promotion of justice and care of the poor. Priorities must be determined and maintained, but one without the other falls short of biblical principle and example. As Harvie M. Conn has forcefully pointed out, evangelism in the biblical sense means doing justice while at the same time preaching grace. Only then does the Holy Spirit—who in former ages moved the prophets in their ringing defense of the poor, and who shone through the healing, feeding ministry of Jesus and led the early church to establish diaconal ministries—communicate through the modern church the message of the forgiving and compassionate God.

A Pastor-Evangelist in Lima, Peru

Pastoring an evangelical church in the South American country of Peru can be a dangerous occupation. Violent attacks have been made in recent years against Protestant churches, and many pastors have been killed. In defense of their people, church leaders have dared to speak out against the terrorists, some of whom have direct government connections, and pastors live in daily fear of reprisals for their defense of the innocent. Evangelical churches have plunged into relief ministries, gathering food, money, medicine, and clothing for the hundreds of widows and orphans left as victims of the violence.

Pastor Pedro Arana leads a Presbyterian congregation in Lima, and he is actively involved in church planting in other areas. He is deeply committed to the organized church, pastoral care of the members, leadership development in the congregations, and vigorous evangelism of a kind that multiplies believers and churches. He blends ministry to the soul and body and trains his members in the same way. His letters are filled with evidence of pastoral ministry of the highest order, combining care and development of believers with evangelistic outreach and compassionate ministries among the poor. What follows is taken from one of Pastor Arana's recent letters:

> I have a pastoral purpose in mentioning the severe weather we have been having, because the weather has been affecting the shape of our ministry. Last week we received a visit from two ex-convicts asking help to buy medicine and clothing. Both were released from prison five months ago. They have no documents, house, job, nor any means to get work. One of them sleeps in abandoned cars, despite the cold weather. What, they asked us, could we offer them? Of course we offered the gospel of salvation. We also offered medical care. One of our deacons took them for a meal at a restaurant close to our church. I was reminded of the words, "You did it unto me." But

as time passes, a more striking verse is sinking in: "When you have done all that you were told, say, 'Useless servants are we, because we have only done that which we should have done.'"

A widow with three children, ages twelve, ten, and four, all of them injured in some way by the floods in the north, made contact with our church. They currently reside in a desert-like section of the city of Lima, without water, electricity or toilet. They live in a small room made of wood with a straw mat as their roof. This does not protect them from the nightly dew which in turn has caused the children to be sick for several weeks. We supplied them with food and blankets, but what they really need is a room made of durable materials to be built on donated land. The deacons of the church have taken action, and we are in the midst of carrying out plans.

In each of these cases the church has provided immediate solutions. But the most effective kind of relief, that of creating sources of employment, has been left uncompleted. We have not been able to take the next step toward development. The brethren who earlier accompanied me in both evangelism and social work now think that we should not take on more projects and programs. But it seems to me that social transformation will then remain only a dream.

There are basic needs that are growing in size and number each day, such as food, housing, clothing, health, education and jobs. I believe we should ask the Lord to stimulate our imagination in order to create new sources of work here in town and in the rural areas. It will be difficult, but not impossible. There are several brethren who are taxi drivers and mechanics, but unemployed. We could start with two projects, the first one being a taxi service. Other brethren in the interior of the country have farms producing coffee, cocoa and wood, and they are being exploited by the "middle men." If they had a truck, it would solve their problem. We have to organize the unemployed people or their needs will continue to go unmet.

Should I start this task? A work like this is a lot to handle for a local congregation. I find myself looking for God's direction just like I did in the early years of my ministry. How to carry out an urban pastoral ministry with so many spiritual, emotional, moral and material needs all around? How does one know how to start?

Pastor Arana has made many good starts, as the correspondence between us reveals. He preaches and teaches regularly in four locations, developing young congregations in each place. He is busy training elders and deacons for each church and is involved in numerous programs of his denomination. And he has put his life on the line by identifying with other pastors in their protest against violence from terrorist and government forces. He is, in short, a pastor-evangelist, declaring the Word of God, caring for believers, organizing the church for biblical ministries, and actively seeking the lost and wounded, bringing them home. In such people the Christian apostolate lives on.

Index

Accurate information, 87, 127-28. *See also* Accurate picture

Accurate picture, 60, 63, 77, 87, 89, 120, 123. *See also* Accurate information

Actual conditions, 83. *See also* Actual facts; Actual situations

Actual facts, 118, 121. *See also* Actual conditions; Actual situations

Actual growth, 72

Actual obedience, 99

Actual situations, 107. *See also* Actual conditions; Actual facts

Africa, 5, 7, 22, 57, 59, 60, 63, 65, 85, 88, 90, 94, 102-3, 118, 124

Agnostic, 5, 17, 29

American church growth, 92-94, 114

American Society of Missiology, 90-91

Animism, 57-58, 71, 81, 83, 85, 88

Anthropology, 21, 30, 57-58, 71, 75, 81, 84-85

Arn, Winfield, 93, 114

Asia, 3, 5, 22, 60, 81, 86, 88, 102, 111

Association of Evangelical Professors of Missions, 91

Atheist, 5, 17, 29, 60

Atonement, 17, 29, 57

Aymara, 70

Bakke, Ray, 111

Barrett, David, 35, 85

Benjamin, Paul, 2-3

Bible colleges, 1, 8, 12, 18-19, 22, 29, 41, 44, 46, 62, 67, 90, 97, 117, 119-20, 125, 129, 132, 134, 136-37

Biblical imperatives, 44. *See also* Command

Biblical mandate. *See* Command

Biblical soundness, x-xi, 34-39, 41-42, 45, 51, 83. *See also* Correct doctrines; Doctrinal correctness

Biological growth, 43, 117

Blindfolded, 48, 117, 119, 126

Blue collar, 4, 7, 124

Branch (of the church), 34-35, 105, 136

Brazil, 72, 76, 80, 100-101

Bridges of God, The, 66, 106

Brotherhood, 24, 40, 103, 115

Buddhism, 57-58, 83

Carey, William, 16, 102

Cho, Paul Yonggi, 102, 129-30, 134

Christensen, Mark, 18

Christianization, 65, 70, 128

Christianize, 3, 20, 86, 92, 97, 112

Church Growth Bulletin, 75, 85, 92

Cities, 5, 18, 26, 35, 77, 83, 96-97, 111-12, 114, 118, 122-23, 129, 133

Command, x, 1, 7, 13-20, 22, 29, 53, 67, 77, 83, 91, 103, 110, 115, 121, 123, 128. *See also* Biblical imperative

Communicate, 1, 6, 39, 57

Communicator, x, 6

Comparative religion, 58, 84

Conciliar, 75

Confucianism, 57, 83

Congress on the Church's Worldwide Mission, 72, 86

Conn, Harvie, 2, 122

Contemporary Theologies of Mission, 100

Conversion growth, 43-44, 117

Convert, 30, 117

Correct doctrine, 1, 6, 25, 27-29, 41. *See also* Biblical soundness; Doctrinal correctness